20,000 Words in Spanish, *in 20 Minutes!*

468
M475t

by

Charles Mazal-Cami

i

Copyright © 1994 by Charles Mazal-Cami

ISBN 0-9630572-3-5

First Edition, 1991
1st Printing: 10/91
2nd Printing: 3/92
Second Edition,1994
1st Printing: 11/94

Published by

Palabra Press
13423 Blanco Road, Suite 232
San Antonio, TX 78216

PRINTED IN THE UNITED STATES OF AMERICA

This book is dedicated to my wife, Roz, who learned Spanish the *hard* way (without this book) and whose approval and encouragement made writing it a delightful experience.

A Note from the Author:

It is with a great deal of personal satisfaction that I put the final touches on this, the Second Edition of "20,000 Words in Spanish, *in 20 Minutes!*". If the success of the original edition is any indication, then I know that you are going to love this book! Selling only by word of mouth among readers, many of whom have written unsolicited letters expressing their delight with the book, the first edition quickly sold out and, just as quickly, moved through a second printing. In support of the thousands of readers who approved of this method for learning Spanish, I have diligently reworked the book and hopefully made it even more fun to read and easier to understand. The premise, of course, remains unchanged: it is intended to initiate you, the reader, into Spanish with lightning speed, so quickly in fact that you will be amazed with yourself! Perhaps your new-found confidence will encourage you to pursue the language further. Letters from readers have convinced me that "20,000 Words.." has proved its merit to college students, career professionals, travelers and the just merely curious. I am hoping that you, too, will benefit from this book and perhaps find the time to write the publisher and express your views on this Second Edition.

Charles Mazal-Cami

PROLOGUE

This book is about words. In order to learn a language, you must know words, and not just their pronunciation: you must know their meaning. Even a one-word sentence can be a handy thing to know if you are trying to communicate with someone who speaks a different language than your own!

Putting words together in another language to communicate a more complex thought than simply "go" or "come" takes some time, and lots of practice, but it becomes a very much less difficult task if you know a few thousand words in the language, and know their meaning and pronunciation.

This book will teach you thousands of words in Spanish, not just common everyday words, but also scientific and medical terms, obscure complex words, adjectives, verbs, nouns and adverbs. The wonderful part about this new method is that the only language you need to know in order to learn Spanish, is English (and you already know English!)

If you would like to read a synopsis of what this book will teach you, turn to the final Chapter 20 (Roundup). Besides having learned thousands of Spanish words, you will also have learned how to recognize word genders, how to conjugate verbs and how to form simple sentences.

If you are contemplating taking a course in Spanish, you will derive a remarkable advantage if you read this book first! By doing so, you will begin your course with a vocabulary of thousands of Spanish words and a working knowledge of some of the basic grammatical rules. It will greatly simplify the sometimes tedious task of learning a new language and you will have gained considerable confidence that you can learn Spanish!

Should you travel to a Spanish-speaking country after reading this book, you won't need to fumble through a miniature dictionary to find the right word. You will know the right word, and you will know how to pronounce it!

In this book you will find many hundreds of word examples. It is not intended that you read each and all of these examples, as it would obviously take you more than twenty minutes to do that! Concentrate your effort in learning each of the Rules that are set forth and for each Rule that you learn, you will have learned many hundreds, or even thousands, of words in Spanish!

Learning another language should be fun, not work! To realize, all of a sudden, that you actually know words in that language, that you know what they mean and how to pronounce them, how to read and write them and that you will likely never forget them (unless you forget how to speak English) should quicken your breath and encourage you to keep learning!

One thing that should be clear: this book is a key to Spanish. It has been designed to teach you quickly and simply that you can learn a new language. With a tiny bit of practice, you will be able to communicate your thoughts to a Spanish-speaking individual, perhaps not grammatically complete, but essently correct. With this new-found confidence, you will want to pursue the language further because you will know that just about any essential word (within the scope of the easy Rules you will learn) that comes to you in English, you will be able to translate to Spanish.

One more thing. It is wonderful to know how to read, speak and understand thousands of words in Spanish. But you must also know how to prounouce them properly, so that you can speak confidently. The first Chapter is about Spanish pronunciation. Read it carefully and refer back to it often, until the Spanish pronunciation of the vowels comes naturally!

Have fun, and *Welcome to Español!*

Table of Contents

Spanish, in Mexico, is rich in words from ancient native tongues, to the delight of those who have grown up in that Country and to the consternation of those who would wish to "speak like a native". Words like "Guajolote" (derived from the Náhuatl word "Guajolótl", which means "turkey"), or "Paranganacutirimícuaro", the name of a small village in the State of Michoacán, send most word-root seekers into a spiral fall! The enrichment of the *Mexican* Spanish by its natives is possibly unique in the world, in that so many different cultures have had an influence in the official language of the Country.

Many words in *Mexican* Spanish derive from Náhuatl, Chichimecan, Mayan, Zapotec, Tarahumaran and other ancient languages, most of which are still spoken today in their pure form by the native inhabitants. With the exception of the word "Zopilote", derived from the Náhuatl word "Zopilotl", we won't be touching on this interesting part of the language. (This word, incidentally, appears on Page 98)

CHAPTER ONE

PRONUNCIATION

If you had recently arrived in an English-speaking country and were faced with having to learn to read and write the language, you would be faced with a monumental task. Words like "knight", and "knowledge" and "pheasant" would be enough to discourage even the most determined student. Consider yourself lucky that you have already *learned* the language! In English, each of the vowels, and many of the consonants, have different ways of being pronounced, and for just about any "rule" there are a half-a-dozen "exceptions".

So, don't despair! Spanish is a cinch to read, write and pronounce. It is pronounced exactly as it is written and, conversely, it is written just as it is pronounced. Perhaps that is why there are no torturous "spelling bees" in Spanish-speaking countries: if you can *prounounce* a word, you can *spell it out* correctly! You see, in Spanish, *every letter* is pronounced, which is why it is so simple to convert vocal Spanish to written words.

The *most important* part of spoken Spanish is the *pronunciation of the vowels.* It is this one aspect of Spanish that separates the tourist from the native. If you *pronounce* the language correctly, it will encourage you to *speak* it confidently!

Spanish pronunciation of the vowels differs from that in English. You will need to rework your brain cells a bit in order to get it right but the *good news* is that in Spanish, like in English, there are only five vowels. The even *better news* is that they are always pronounced exactly the same way. Compared to English where, for example, the "a" must be pronounced differently for "apple" than it is for "acorn" or "awful", you will find that Spanish is a snap!

Although the clock is ticking, let's take a moment to have a look at this *most important* part of Spanish pronunciation. We will still have plenty of time left to learn the thousands upon thousands of Spanish words you were promised on the cover of the book!

THE VOWELS

In Spanish, there are five vowels:

$$\boxed{\textbf{a, e, i, o, u}}$$

Learn these five sounds and you will be able to pronounce any word in Spanish correctly!

"a"   Pronounced "aah", as in "f<u>a</u>r" or "f<u>a</u>ther"

"e"   Pronounced "eh", as in "m<u>e</u>n" or "M<u>e</u>xico"

"i"   Pronounced "ee" as in "fr<u>ee</u>" or "s<u>ee</u>"

"o"   Pronounced "oh" as in "C<u>o</u>ke". It's a very curt sound. Place your mouth as if to pronounce "OH" but don't move your jaw or lips, and force a quick, short grunt. It's like taking the"w" off of "m<u>o</u>w".

"u"   Pronounced "<u>oo</u>h", as in "m<u>oo</u>", or "t<u>oo</u>". When *preceded* by a "q", (unless the "u" is followed by an "a"), the "u" is silent. More on this later (See Quirk # 7)

Every language has its own intrinsicacies and Spanish is no exception. Apart from the pronunciation of the vowels, there are other characteristics that make Spanish *different* from English. Thankfully, as you will see in later chapters, there are also many things that make it the *same!* We will refer to these differences as *quirks*. They constitute an integral part of Spanish pronunciation and at some point you will need to learn them. However, there is no need to memorize them right now because in later chapters we will refer back to them whenever they appear. If you aren't in a race with the clock then, go ahead, take a look!

Quirk # 1: *The Spanish stealth letter.*
The "h" is silent (not pronounced) unless it is preceded by a "c", in which case it sounds like "ch" in English [i.e. **Chicken, Charlie**]. Hercules is pronounced EHR-COO-LESS

Quirk # 2: *I smile when I'm jappy.*
The "j" in Spanish is pronounced like an "h" in English [i.e. Happy]. José (Joseph, in Spanish) is pronounced HO-SEH. There is no "J" sound in Spanish. Instead, substitute "y" for "j" - Major, in Spanish, is Mayor.

Quirk # 3: *Of yams and llamas.*
There are two ways of achieving the **"y"** sound in Spanish and essentially it is pronounced in Spanish as you would in English (as in Mayan). It's called "i Griega" (Greek i"). Some words achieve the "y" sound through the use of the double-L ["**ll**"] which is also considered a single letter in the Spanish alphabet (following "L") and pronounced EH-YEH. The **llama**, that delightful Peruvian herbivore, is pronounced "LA-MA" by English-speaking folks but is pronounced "YA-MA" in Spanish. Standing alone and pronounced "EE", the letter "y", in Spanish, means "and".

Quirk # 4: *Wilhelm, Wasser & Wunderbar.*
You will find it in the Alphabet but there is no "w" in modern Spanish with the exception of some "foreign" words, mostly of German extraction. Some academicians call this letter the double-V and others insist that it is the double-U. In either case, if you run across it in Spanish, pronounce it like you would in English. There is no "wh" combination in Spanish.

Quirk # 5: *You could have phooled me!*
There is no **"ph"** combination in Spanish. If it *sounds* like an **"f"**, it *is* an "f". [i.e., "ph obia", in Spanish is "fobia"] The same applies to other tricky English combinations like **"kn"**, **"pf"**, **"pn"**, **"gh"**, **"wh"** or **"cz"**. *Isn't that a relief?*

Quirk # 6: *Fuel up at the Espanish gas estation.*
Words that in English begin with "Sp", "Sc" or "St", in Spanish these are *preceded* by an **"E"** [i.e., **Sp**ecial becomes **Esp**ecial]. That's why it is called **Esp**añol!

Quirk # 7: *Tie it in a not.* (Also see Quirk # 5)
There is no "k" in Spanish except in some "foreign" words like **K**oala, although it is in the alphabet. When you run across it, pronounce it like a "k" in English. The **"k"** sound is achieved in Spanish with the **"Q"** when it is followed by either "ue" or "ui". In both cases, the "u" is silent. "Que" is pronounced KEH and "Qui" is pronounced KEE. When "Q" is followed by "ua" **(qua)**, *both* vowels are pronounced, resulting in KOO-AH. "Torque" in Spanish is *also* "Torque" but is pronounced TOR-KEH. It means the same thing, too. (Also see Quirk # 8)

Quirk # 8: *Spanish is cimple.*
As in English, the **"c"** sounds like a "k" *unless* it precedes an **"i"** or an **"e"**, in which case it sounds like an "s". ("Taco" is pronounced TAH-KOE and "Gracias" is pronounced GRA-SEE-AHS - which means thank you).

Quirk # 9: *Mexico, Texas and Xochimilco.*
The **"x"** in Spanish is a mess. When it is between two vowels, it is pronounced like an "h" in English. ("Mexico" is pronounced MEH-HEE-COE). If it is followed by a consonant, it is pronounced like an "x" ("Texto", Spanish for "Text", is pronounced TEX-TOE). Sometimes, in words derived from native languages such as Náhuatl or Chichimecan, it is pronounced like an **"s"** or even as **"sh"**.

Quirk # 10: *The Grand Cañon.*

In Spanish, there is an **"ñ"**. Alphabetically, it follows the "n" but the pronunciation of this odd letter is different. In English, you would pronounce it EN-YEH and it is equivalent to the **"ny"** sound, as in "Canyon". There is a capital **"Ñ"** and a lower case **"ñ"**. The Spanish word "niño" (boy) is pronounced NEEN-YO.

Quirk # 11: *A half-thozen, glazed thoughnuts.*

You guessed it. The **"d"** in Spanish, is prounounced like a soft "th", as in "**th**ose" (*not* as in path), and a good reason for there not to be any double-d's in Español!

Quirk # 12: *Antibiotics kill herms.*

A **"g"**, when followed by an **"e"**, is pronounced like an "h" in English. Otherwise, it's just a "g", as in "garden".

Quirk # 13: *Everything else is the zame.*

The **"z"** in Spanish is always pronounced like an "s", as in "set". (Unless you're in Madrid where they pronounce it "th", as in lithp). Plain and zimple.   OK, get ready, get zet, go!

THE CONSONANTS

You will be delighted to learn that, *except as noted in the Quirks*, the consonants are pronounced in Spanish just as you would in English. That is, a B, an M or a P are still just B, M and P, and this applies to all the rest of the consonants. In Spanish words, *every letter is pronounced* and you won't come across any strange stuff like "phlegm", "night", "chrome" or "gnat". As noted, if it *sounds* like an "f", it *is* an "f" and that goes for all those other strange letter combinations.

Also, with the exception of the double-l (**"ll"** - Quirk # 3), the double-c (**"cc"**) and the double-r (**"rr"**),
there are no *repeated* consonants in Spanish!

Out the window go the double *F*'s, double *G*'s, double *M*'s, double *N*'s, double *P*'s, double *S*'s and double *T*'s that haunt English.
[i.e., "afford", "aggravate", "emmanate", "penny", "apply", "essay", "attorney"]

One **"f"**, **"g"**, **"m"**, **"n"**, **"p"**, **"s"** or **"t"**
is all that is needed.

So much for the consonants.

STRESSES and ACCENTS

Everything you ever wanted to know about accents
(but were afraid to ask). You don't *really* need to know this yet but it will certainly help your pronunciation! There are no intelligible rules for stressing certain syllables in English words and you pretty well need to learn each word individually. In Spanish, however, it's either
Rule 1, Rule 2 or neither of them.
Look how simple it really is:

RULE I:
A word ending in N, S or a vowel receives *stress* on the *next to last* Syllable (except words *ending* in ...ion). Examples:

Spanish		*English*
den**tis**ta	(*stress* **tis**)	dentist
po**si**ble	(*stress* **si**)	posible
argu**men**to	(*stress* **men**)	argument
primi**ti**vo	(*stress* **ti**)	primitive
pru**den**te	(*stress* **den**)	prudent
glo**rio**so	(*stress* **rio**)	glorious

Charles Mazal-Cami

RULE II:

When a word does *not* end in N, S or a vowel, it receives *stress* on the *last* syllable: Examples:

Spanish		*English*
pos**tal**	(*stress* **tal**)	postal
cervi**cal**	(*stress* **cal**)	cervical
trac**tor**	(*stress* **tor**)	tractor
circu**lar**	(*stress* **lar**)	circular
capi**tal**	(*stress* **tal**)	capital
espectacu**lar**	(stress **lar**)	spectacular

RULE III:

Any word that does not follow either RULE I or RULE II is an *irregular* word and therefor must have a *written* stress, that is, it must have an *accent.*
Words ending in **...ión** receive an accent on the last syllable (always over the vowel). Examples:

Spanish		*English*
re**pú**blica	re-**pú**-bli-ca	republic
na**ción**	na-**ción**	nation
lógico	**ló**-gi-co	logical
fa**ná**tico	fa-**ná**-ti-co	fanatic
pa**sión**	pa-**sión**	passion

That covers most of it. *Don't panic!* You will see as we go along that it isn't as difficult as it might appear

A (TINY) BIT OF GRAMMAR

We will get into more grammar later on in the book, once you have learned the thousands of words that you were promised.
However, this curious fact you should know:
Spanish is, in certain ways, a mirror-image of English.

In English, the adjective comes *before* the noun.
[i.e. "*large* house"]

In Spanish, the adjective comes *after* the noun.
[i.e. "casa *grande*"]

If you stop to think about it, it makes a lot of sense.
You don't need to wait around for all the adjectives
before knowing what it is you're talking about. *i.e.*:
"I couldn't hold on to the *squiggly, slimey, wriggling, jumping, slippery*
fish!"

THE SPANISH ALPHABET

The Alphabet in Spanish is much like the alphabet in English. It's called
the "**ALFABETO**", and includes the three extra letters we have
reviewed (CH, LL and Ñ) Remember that, although the "K" and the
"W" form part of the *Alfabeto*, there are very few words in Spanish that
include these letters and most of these are "foreign" words.
This is what the *Alfabeto* looks like:

A B C **CH** D E F G H I J K L **LL**
M N Ñ O P Q R S T U V W X Y Z.

THE RULES
(How this book works)

A bit of History: English and Spanish share an enormous common
ground. Both languages are derived from ancient languages, primarily
what we will call here Indo-European. English was developed from
many more derivatives of Indo-European than was Spanish, but both
share a considerable influence of Latin, Hellenic, Arabic and other
Mediterranean languages. The principle departure is Germanic, which
has had much influence in modern English but very little in modern
Spanish. However, it will astound you to learn just how many words in
English are *practically* the same as their Spanish counterparts, with only
a slight difference in spelling, and how many are *exactly* the same!

The Method: Words that are similar in two languages are technically known as *cognates.* These words might have slight differences in their spelling, usually in the *ending* of the words, but since they have derived from the same *roots*, the meaning is nearly always the same. There are thousands upon thousands of cognates in the English language and those which will occupy us here are English-*Spanish* cognates. In the pages ahead, you will find that by simply altering the *ending* of an English word, you will know the Spanish equivalent of that word. In some cases, even the ending is the same!

In order to catalog these endings in an easy-to-understand fashion, we have referred to these different word-endings as **RULES** and they appear *roughly* in the order of their accuracy. Some RULES are more accurate than others; that is, there are fewer *exceptions.* Also, some RULES apply to a much larger number of English words than do others. Those that apply to the largest number of words are listed here as **MAJOR RULES** and those having fewer number of English equivalents are listed as **MINOR RULES**.

The first fourteen RULES apply to far more than *twenty thousand English words* (hence the title of this book) and are known here as the MAJOR RULES. Thousands *more* word-endings are covered under the MINOR RULES. **Since you already *know* the words, because you speak English, all you need to learn are the RULES!**

This book is the result of considerable research and is intended to teach you - as promised- virtually *thousands* of words in Spanish by using your knowledge of *English.* If you are an average reader, you will *"learn" hundreds of words per minute!* You will know common words and obscure ones as well, including nouns, verbs, adjectives and adverbs. The extent of your *English* vocabulary is the only limitation to how many *Spanish* words you will know! It is not within the scope of this book to teach you grammatical usage beyond recognizing words genders, conjugating verbs, using articles, and forming simple sentences in Spanish. It *is* intended to teach you enough useful words to be able to communicate in the language. When you finish this book, you should deservedly marvel at your new-found knowledge and you should want to pursue learning the language fluently.

You are ready now to learn some Español!

"The ice borrows its substances from the river, it is indeed the actual water of the river itself - and yet it is not the river. A child, seeing the ice, thinks that the river exists no more, that its course has been arrested. But this is only an ilusion. Under the layer of ice, the river continues to flow down to the plain. Should the ice break, one sees the water suddenly bubble up as it goes gushing and murmuring on its way. This is an image of the stream of language. The written tongue is the film of ice upon its waters; the stream which still flows under the ice that imprisons it is the popular and natural language; the cold which produces the ice and would fain restrain the flood is the stabilizing action exerted by grammarians and pedagogues; and the sunbeam which gives language its liberty is the indomitable force of life, triumphing over rules, and breaking the fetters of tradition."*

*J.Vendryes, *Language: A Linguistic Introduction to History*, translated by Paul Radin (New York, 1925)

Charles Mazal-Cami

CHAPTER TWO

THE **TION** RULE
(Major)

This Rule applies to those words in **English** with two or more syllables
that *end* **with the letters**

....tion

To translate them into **Spanish**, we will *substitute* the ending with

....ción

As an example, the English word **Nation** is the Spanish word **Nación**
(pronounced nah-see-on)

**Remember that we will *write* an accent on the last syllable
of Spanish words ending with ...ión** (see Page 6)

Here are some purposely-chosen <u>uncommon</u> words as examples:

English		*Spanish*	*Helpful Reminders*
....tion	**=**	**....ción**	
Administra**tion**..........		Administra**ción**	
Applica**tion**................		Aplica**ción**	[Only 1 P!]
Benedic**tion**................		Benedic**ción**	

English	Spanish	Helpful Reminders
Bifurcation...............	Bifurcación	
Classification...........	Clasificación	[Only 1 S!]
Conservation...........	Conservación	
Distribution.............	Distribución	
Embarcation............	Embarcación	
Education................	Educación	
Frustration...............	Frustración	
Fabrication..............	Fabricación	
Gravitation..............	Gravitación	[Quirk # 12]
Gasification.............	Gasificación	[Quirk # 12]
Hibernation............	Hibernación	[Quirk # 1!]
Hospitalization........	Hospitalización	[Quirk # 1!]
Installation..............	Instalación	[note only 1 "L"]
Instruction...............	Instrucción	[Quirk # 8!]
Justification.............	Justificación	[Quirk # 2 & # 8!]
Jubillation...............	Jubilación	[Quirk # 2!]
Lamination..............	Laminación	
Laceration...............	Laceración	
Mechanization.........	Mecanización	[Quirk # 8!]
Manipulation...........	Manipulación	
Narration.................	Narración	
Nation.....................	Nación	
Occupation..............	Ocupación	[Quirk # 8! Only 1 C!]
Oscillation...............	Oscilación	[Quirk # 8! Only 1 L!]
Palpation.................	Personificación	
Ratification..............	Ratificación	
Ramification............	Ramificación	
Sensation................	Sensación	
Salvation.................	Salvación	
Station....................	Estación	[Quirk # 6!]
Transportation..........	Transportación	
Transition................	Transición	
Violation.................	Violación	
Ventilation.............	Ventilación	

As a simple exercise, fill in the Spanish translations for the following English words:

(Don't forget the accent!)

Adula**tion**......................._____

Corrup**tion**....................._____

Evacua**tion**...................._____

Nutri**tion**......................._____

Palpita**tion**...................._____

Specula**tion**...................._____ [Quirk # 6!]

Well, how *ABOUT* it? You are
reading and *writing* **SPANISH!**

With this Rule, you have just learned nearly
TWO THOUSAND words in Spanish!

Notable Exceptions:

English	Spanish
Carnation	Clavel
Caution	Precaución
Temptation	Tentación
Translation	Traducción

> **For those English words in this Rule that you would pluralize by adding an "s" [i.e. Installa*tions*] you simply add "es" to the Spanish translation [i.e. Instala*ciónes*]**

If you are surprised at how simple that was, then you are in for many more pleasant surprises in the chapters to come! This book has been designed to initiate you *quickly* to a "foreign" language and to get you into conversing in Spanish confidently. Once you have learned thousands of words in Spanish, it makes it much easier to learn the *grammar*! Some of the basics are covered in later Chapters in simple, easy-to-understand terms that will give you a head-start. Be sure to *practice the Spanish pronunciation of the vowels* as you read along!

CHAPTER THREE

THE ATE RULE

(Major)

This Rule applies to those words in **English** *with two or more syllables* that *end* with the letters

....ate

To translate them into **Spanish**, we will *substitute* the ending with

....ar

Keep in mind that we are looking for word *endings*. The English verb ATE (past-tense of EAT) *does not apply*, nor do other single-syllable words such as MATE.

As an example, the English verb **Cre<u>ate</u>**, is the Spanish verb **Cre<u>ar</u>**. We need ***verbs*** to *create* sentences, so here are some examples:

(A reminder: pronounce the Spanish vowels correctly!)

English		*Spanish*	*Helpful Reminders*
.....ate	=	**.....ar**	
Articul<u>ate</u>...............		Articul<u>ar</u>	
Ambul<u>ate</u>.................		Ambul<u>ar</u>	
Benefici<u>ate</u>.............		Benefici<u>ar</u>	

English	Spanish	Helpful Reminders
Biannulate..............	Bianular	[only one N!]
Capitulate..............	Capitular	
Conjugate..............	Conjugar	[Quirk # 2!]
Corrugate..............	Corrugar	
Defoliate..............	Defoliar	
Donate..............	Donar	
Elevate..............	Elevar	
Emmulate..............	Emular	[only one M!]
Fabricate..............	Fabricar	
Fluctuate..............	Fluctuar	
Formulate..............	Formular	
Germinate..............	Germinar	[G pron. like H, Quirk # 12!]
Graduate..............	Graduar	[G as in English, Quirk # 12!]
Habituate..............	Habituar	[Quirk # 1!]
Hallucinate..............	Halucinar	[H is silent, one L]
Illuminate..............	Iluminar	[only one L!]
Imitate..............	Imitar	
Initiate..............	Iniciar	[C for T!]
Jubilate..............	Jubilar	[Quirk # 2!]
Jugulate..............	Jugular	[Quirk # 2!]
Lacerate..............	Lacerar	[Quirk # 8]
Lactate..............	Lactar	
Manipulate..............	Manipular	
Masticate..............	Masticar	
Modulate..............	Modular	
Navigate..............	Navegar	[note different spelling]
Necessitate..............	Necesitar	[only one S!]
Obligate..............	Obligar	
Obviate..............	Obviar	
Participate..............	Participar	
Precipitate..............	Precipitar	
Quadruplicate..........	Cuadruplicar	[Quirk # 8!]
Quintuplicate..........	Quintuplicar	[Quirk # 7!]
Radiate..............	Radiar	
Reciprocate..........	Reciprocar	
Segregate..............	Segregar	
Simulate..............	Simular	

Charles Mazal-Cami

English	Spanish	Helpful Reminders
Situate....................	Situar	
Terminate..............	Terminar	
Tolerate.................	Tolerar	
Ulcerate.................	Ulcerar	
Ultimate.................	Ultimar	
Validate.................	Validar	
Variate..................	Variar	

OK. Now a try a few on your own:

Congregate...........	_____	
Contemplate..........	_____	
Delegate..............	_____	
Extricate..............	_____	
Innovate..............	_____	[one N!]
Meditate..............	_____	

If you have an average command of *English*, you have just learned *another* thousand or so words in *Spanish!*

Congratulations!

Now the bad news:

One notable exeption to this rule is the verb Congratulate. Although Congratular is *grammatically* correct it is, sadly, in disuse. The accepted, popular translation is *Felicitar*. Congratulation, therefore, is Felicitación! [see ...tion Rule]. The plural, Congratulations (as we learned in the last Chapter) is **Felicitaciones!**

Each time you learn a Rule, think of a few words in English with that ending and translate them into Spanish applying what you have just learned. Say them out loud, and check your pronunciation against what you have learned in Chapter One, *particularly* with regard to the pronunciation of the *vowels*. It might be confusing, at first, to remember that the "i" is pronounced "ee", or that the "u" is pronounced "oo". Take heart in the fact that the vowels are *always* pronounced the same way in Spanish! The "[Helpful Reminders]" along the word listings mostly refer to the Quirks in Chapter One, and also remind you that, with the exception of the "ll", "rr" and "cc", *there are no double-consonants in Spanish!*

CHAPTER FOUR

THE IZE RULE

(Major)

This Rule applies to those words in **English** that *end* with the letters

....ize

To translate them into **Spanish**, we will *substitute* the ending with

....izar

As an example, the English word Real<u>ize</u> is the Spanish word Real<u>**izar**</u>

The "Z" in Spanish is pronounced like an "S"
(as in **Song**)
[See Quirk # 13]
In the Spanish translation, the last syllable (*ar*) receives *stress*.
(See "Accents", Rule II, Chapter One)
These words are all verbs.

Some more examples:

English	*Spanish*	*Helpful Reminders*
.....ize	**.....izar**	
Amort<u>ize</u>.................	Amort<u>**izar**</u>	
Anal<u>ize</u>....................	Anal<u>izar</u>	
Botan<u>ize</u>.................	Botan<u>izar</u>	
Brutal<u>ize</u>.................	Brutal<u>izar</u>	

English	Spanish	Helpful Reminders
Catalize.................	Catalizar	
Cauterize...............	Cauterizar	
Deodorize................	Deodorizar	
Detonize.................	Detonizar	
Editorialize.............	Editorializar	
Equalize..................	Equalizar	["Q" pron. like "K"!]
Familiarize..............	Familiarizar	
Federalize..............	Federalizar	
Galvanize................	Galvanizar	[Pron. like "G"-Quirk # 12]
Glamorize...............	Glamorizar	[Pron. like "G"-Quirk # 12]
Habitualize.............	Habitualizar	["H" is silent!]
Harmonize..............	Harmonizar	["H" is silent!]
Individualize...........	Individualizar	
Initialize.................	Inicializar	[a "C" sounds like a C!]
Jovialize.................	Jovializar	[Quirk # 2!]
Legalize.................	Legalizar	
Liberalize...............	Liberalizar	
Materialize.............	Materializar	
Mobilize.................	Mobilizar	
Nebulize.................	Nebulizar	
Neutralize...............	Neutralizar	
Patronize.................	Patronizar	
Penalize.................	Penalizar	
Tantalize................	Tantalizar	
Vulcanize...............	Vulcanizar	

Try another exercise on your own. Fill in the blanks:

Capital**ize**...............	_____	
Industrial**ize**...........	_____	
Modern**ize**.............	_____	
Special**ize**..............	_____	[Quirk # 6!]
Trivial**ize**................	_____	

Chalk up *another thousand words*, or so, to your Spanish vocabulary!
Admit it, you know a lot of Spanish already.
And you will soon learn a lot more!

Charles Mazal-Cami

CHAPTER FIVE

THE **AL** RULE
(Major)

This Rule applies to those words in **English** *with two or more syllables*
that *end* with the letters

....al

To translate them into **Spanish**, we will *substitute* the ending with

....al
(simple enough?)

English words ending in ....<u>si</u>al or ....<u>ti</u>al that *sound* like "S" are
translated to Spanish by using the ending ....<u>ci</u>al.
In Spanish, when "c" precedes an "i", it is pronounced like an "s"
(see Quirk # 8)

As an example, the *English* word **Par<u>ti</u>al** is the *Spanish* word **Par<u>ci</u>al**.
The *English* word **Horten<u>si</u>al** is the *Spanish* word **Horten<u>ci</u>al**.

Otherwise, the spelling will be the same (observing the Quirks)

English words ending in ....<u>ti</u>al in which the "t" *sounds* like "t"
(as in Bestial), are spelled the *same* in Spanish (Bestial)

Here are (a lot) more examples:

English		Spanish	Helpful Reminders
English		_Spanish_	_Helpful Reminders_

....al   =   **....al**

Abdomin**al**...............	Abdomin**al**	
Aboriginal................	Aboriginal	
Accessorial..............	Accesorial	[Quirk # 8!; only 1 S]
Accidental...............	Accidental	
Actuarial................	Actuarial	
Administerial...........	Administerial	
Alluvial..................	Aluvial	[Only 1 L!]
Ambisexual..............	Ambisexual	
Angelical................	Angelical	
Annual...................	Anual	[Only 1 N!]
Antisocial................	Antisocial	
Antiviral..................	Antiviral	
Arboreal..................	Arboreal	
Arterial...................	Arterial	
Asexual...................	Asexual	
Astral......................	Astral	
Aural......................	Aural	
Axial.......................	Axial	
Bacterial.................	Bacterial	
Baronial..................	Baronial	
Basal......................	Basal	
Bestial....................	Bestial	
Bilateral.................	Bilateral	
Bifocal....................	Bifocal	
Binocular................	Binocular	
Bipolar....................	Bipolar	
Bisexual..................	Bisexual	
Brutal.....................	Brutal	
Capital....................	Capital	
Carnal.....................	Carnal	
Casual....................	Casual	
Caudal....................	Caudal	
Celestial.................	Celestial	(also Celeste)
Central...................	Central	

English	Spanish	Helpful Reminders
Centrifugal..............	Centrifugal	
Cereal.....................	Cereal	
Cerebral.................	Cerebral	
Cervical..................	Cervical	
Coaxial...................	Coaxial	
Cogenial.................	Cogenial	
Colonial.................	Colonial	
Colossal.................	Colosal	[Only 1 S!]
Commercial.............	Comercial	[Only 1 M!]
Communal..............	Comunal	[Only 1 M!]
Continental.............	Continental	
Cordial...................	Cordial	
Corporal.................	Corporal	
Corpuscular.............	Corpuscular	
Coradial.................	Coradial	
Corral....................	Corral	
Cortical..................	Cortical	
Cranial...................	Cranial	
Credential..............	Credencial	[Note C for T!]
Criminal.................	Criminal	
Crystal...................	Cristal	[I for Y!]
Crucial...................	Crucial	
Cultural..................	Cultural	
Decimal..................	Decimal	
Dental....................	Dental	
Dextral...................	Dextral	
Diagonal.................	Diagonal	
Dictatorial..............	Dictatorial	
Differential.............	Diferencial	[Note C for T & 1 F!]
Digital...................	Digital	
Dimensional............	Dimensional	
Distal.....................	Distal	
Dominical...............	Dominical	
Duodecimal.............	Duodecimal	
Duodenal................	Duodenal	
Electoral.................	Electoral	
Elemental...............	Elemental	
Epidural.................	Epidural	

English	Spanish	Helpful Reminders
Equatorial...............	Ecuatorial	[Note C for Q!]
Equilateral..............	Equilateral	
Essential................	Esencial	[Note C for T & 1 S]
Eternal...................	Eternal	(also Eterno)
Evangelical.............	Evangelical	
Extralegal...............	Extralegal	
Extramarital............	Extramarital	
Extramural..............	Extramural	
Facial....................	Facial	
Fatal.....................	Fatal	
Federal..................	Federal	
Festival..................	Festival	
Filial.....................	Filial	
Final.....................	Final	
Focal....................	Focal	
Formal...................	Formal	
Fraternal................	Fraternal	
Frontal..................	Frontal	
Fundamental..........	Fundamental	
Funeral..................	Funeral	
Galaxial..................	Galaxial	[also Galáctico]
Genial....................	Genial	[G pron. like H -Quirk # 12!]
Genital...................	Genital	[G pron. like H -Quirk # 12!]
Gradual..................	Gradual	
Harmonial...............	Harmonial	[Quirk # 1]
Hexagonal...............	Hexagonal	
Hibernal.................	Hibernal	[Quirk # 1]
Homosexual.............	Homosexual	[Quirk # 1]
Horizontal..............	Horizontal	[Quirk # 1]
Hospital.................	Hospital	[Quirk # 1]
Ideal.....................	Ideal	
Illegal....................	Ilegal	[Only 1 L!]
Immoral.................	Inmoral	[N for M!]
Imperial.................	Imperial	
Impersonal.............	Inpersonal	[N for M!]
Inaugural................	Inaugural	
Incidental...............	Incidental	

English	Spanish	Helpful Reminders
Individual...............	Individual	
Infernal..................	Infernal	
Initial....................	Inicial	[Note C for T!]
Integral..................	Integral	
Intellectual.............	Intelectual	[Only 1 L!]
International...........	Internacional	[C for T!]
Jovial....................	Jovial	[Quirk # 2!]
Judicial..................	Judicial	[Quirk # 2!]
Labial....................	Labial	
Lacrimal.................	Lagrimal	[Note G for C!]
Lacteal...................	Lacteal	(also Lactea)
Lateral...................	Lateral	
Latitudinal..............	Latitudinal	
Legal.....................	Legal	
Liberal...................	Liberal	
Lineal....................	Lineal	
Literal...................	Literal	
Litoral...................	Litoral	
Local.....................	Local	
Longitudinal.........	Longitudinal	
Madrigal................	Madrigal	
Magisterial.............	Magisterial	
Manual...................	Manual	
Menial...................	Menial	
Marginal................	Marginal	
Marsupial...............	Marsupial	(also Marsupio)
Marital..................	Marital	
Martial..................	Marcial	[Quirk # 8!]
Maternal................	Maternal	(also Materno)
Medieval................	Medieval	
Menstrual...............	Menstrual	
Mental...................	Mental	
Meridional.............	Meridional	
Mezcal...................	Mezcal	
Metal.....................	Metal	
Mineral..................	Mineral	
Mistral...................	Mistral	
Mitral....................	Mitral	

English	Spanish	Helpful Reminders
Modal......................	Modal	
Monaural................	Monaural	
Montreal.................	Montreal	
Monumental............	Monumental	
Moral......................	Moral	
Mortal....................	Mortal	
Mural......................	Mural	
Musical...................	Musical	
Narial.....................	Narial	
Nasal......................	Nasal	
Natal......................	Natal	
National.................	Nacional	
Natural...................	Natural	
Naval......................	Naval	
Nepal......................	Nepal	
Neural....................	Neural	
Neutral..................	Neutral	
Nominal.................	Nominal	
Normal...................	Normal	
Nutritial.................	Nutricial	[Note C for T; Quirk # 8!]
Occidental..............	Occidental	[Quirk # 8!]
Occipital................	Occipital	[Quirk # 8!]
Official..................	Oficial	[Note only 1 F!]
Oral........................	Oral	
Orbital...................	Orbital	
Orchestral..............	Orquestral	[QUE for CH!]
Oriental.................	Oriental	
Original.................	Original	
Parental.................	Pariental	[Note i!]
Parietal..................	Parietal	
Palatial..................	Palacial	[Note C for T; Quirk # 8!]
Pastoral.................	Pastoral	
Paternal.................	Paternal	(also Paterno)
Pectoral.................	Pectoral	
Pedal......................	Pedal	
Pedestal.................	Pedestal	
Penal......................	Penal	

Charles Mazal-Cami

English	Spanish	Helpful Reminders
Pentagonal..............	Pentagonal	
Perinatal.................	Perinatal	
Personal.................	Personal	
Plural......................	Plural	
Portal.....................	Portal	
Primordial..............	Primordial	
Principal.................	Principal	
Proverbial..............	Proverbial	
Provincial...............	Provincial	
Proximal.................	Proximal	
Punctual.................	Puntual	[Note no C!]
Quintal...................	Quintal	
Rabbinical..............	Rabinical	[Only 1 B!]
Racial.....................	Racial	[Quirk # 8]
Radial.....................	Radial	
Recital...................	Recital	
Regional.................	Regional	
Renal......................	Renal	
Residential..............	Residencial	[C for T!]
Residual.................	Residual	(also Residuo)
Rival......................	Rival	
Rural......................	Rural	
Sacerdotal...............	Sacerdotal	
Sectorial.................	Sectorial	
Semental.................	Semental	
Semifinal................	Semifinal	
Semiformal.............	Semiformal	
Sensual...................	Sensual	
Sensational.............	Sensacional	[C for T!]
Sentimental.............	Sentimental	
Serial.....................	Serial	
Sexual....................	Sexual	
Sisal......................	Sisal	
Skeletal.................	Esqueletal	[Quirks # 6 & 7!]
Social....................	Social	
Spatial...................	Espacial	[Quirk # 6!, C for T!]
Special..................	Especial	[Quirk # 6]

English	Spanish	Helpful Reminders
Spinal	Espinal	[E before SP; Quirk # 6!]
Sequential	Secuencial	[Note C for Q!]
Structural	Estructural	[E before ST!]
Subliminal	Subliminal	
Tangential	Tangencial	[Note C for T!]
Temperamental	Temperamental	
Tempestual	Tempestual	
Temporal	Temporal	
Terminal	Terminal	
Testamental	Testamental	
Tetragonal	Tetragonal	
Textual	Textual	
Thermal	Termal	[Note no H!]
Timbal	Timbal	(also Tímbalo)
Topical	Topical	
Torrential	Torrencial	[Note C for T!]
Total	Total	
Tribunal	Tribunal	
Tropical	Tropical	
Umbilical	Umbilical	
Uncial	Uncial	[Quirk # 8!]
Unilateral	Unilateral	
Universal	Universal	
Urticarial	Urticarial	
Usual	Usual	
Vaginal	Vaginal	
Venal	Venal	
Venial	Venial	
Verbal	Verbal	
Vertebral	Vertebral	
Vertical	Vertical	
Vestigial	Vestigial	[G pron. like Eng. "H"]
Vial	Vial	
Viral	Viral	
Virginal	Virginal	
Visual	Visual	
Vocal	Vocal	

There are many, *many* more!
They might *look* like English words, but they are also *Spanish!*
You can double up on what you have just learned, too:
For the plural on the Spanish words above, just add **....es**!
The plural for *Universal,* for example, is *Universal***es**!

Proper *pronunciación* of the Spanish vowels is *everything!*

We can forego the practice session, yes?

Who *said* that you couldn't learn Español?

A few of the exceptions to this Rule, are:

English	Spanish
Continual	Contínuo
Magical	Mágico
Petal	Pétalo
Terrestial	Terréstre

There are possibly many more "exceptions" to the Rules than are put forth in the examples. Those that are listed are the ones which are most common. Remember, however, that the Major Rules, on a percentage basis, have *very few* exceptions and the overwhelming odds are that you will correctly translate English words to Spanish by applying the Rules. In most cases, even the *exceptions* are similar enough to be understood by a Spanish-speaking individual, so you should feel confident that, when you are speaking the words, you are making yourself understood!

CHAPTER SIX

THE IC RULE

(Major)

This Rule applies to those words in **English** that *end* with the letters

....ic

To translate them into **Spanish**, we will *substitute* the ending with

....ico

As an example, the English word Rust<u>ic</u> is the Spanish word Rús<u>tico</u>.

A reminder: this ending is pronounced EE-KO

Rústico, then, is pronounced ROOS-TEE-KO

This Rule applies to many useful words in *Academia*
(Chemistry, Geography, Physics, Medicine, etc.) as well as
common-usage words.

These are *irregular* words and therefor receive
written accents as shown. The *stress*, of course
is on the syllable where the written accent is located.
The accent is always written above the vowel in that syllable.
(See ACCENTS in Chapter One)

Here are some more examples:

English		Spanish	Helpful Reminders
English	=	_Spanish_	_Helpful Reminders_
....ic	=	....ico	
Academi**c**		Académi**co**	
Acidic		Acídico	
Aquatic		Aquático	
Arctic		Ártico[1]	[See Note end of Chapter]
Baltic		Báltico	
Barometric		Barométrico	
Caloric		Calórico	
Caustic		Caústico	
Clinic		Clínica	[Femenine Gender!]
Eccentric		Eccéntrico	
Fanatic		Fanático	
Galactic		Galáctico	
Geographic		Geográfico	[Quirks # 5, 12]
Harmonic		Harmónico	[Quirk # 1]
Hemostatic		Hemostático	[Quirk # 1]
Intrinsic		Intrínsico	
Impiric		Impírico	
Juridic		Jurídico	
Kinetic		Kinético	
Linguistic		Lingüístico	
Logic		Lógica	[Femenine Gender!][2]
Magic		Mágico	
Magnetic		Magnético	
Mimic		Mímico	
Nautic		Náutico	
Nordic		Nórdico	
Ophthalmic		Oftálmico	[Quirk # 5!;T for TH]
Organic		Orgánico	
Orthopedic		Ortopédico	[No TH in Spanish!]
Panic		Pánico	
Plastic		Plástico	
Pragmatic		Pragmático	
Problematic		Problemático	
Quadratic		Cuadrático	[C for Q,Quirk # 7!]

English	Spanish	Helpful Reminders
Quart**ic**	Cuárt**ico**	[C for Q,Quirk # 7!]
Republ**ic**	Repúbl**ica**	[Femenine Gender!] [2]
Rhetor**ic**	Retór**ico**	[No "RH" in Spanish!]
Sept**ic**	Sépt**ico**	
Simplist**ic**	Simplíst**ico**	
Symphon**ic**	Sinfón**ico**	[N for M -Quirk # 5!]
Telegraph**ic**	Telegráf**ico**	[Quirk # 5!]
Ton**ic**	Tón**ico**	
Tox**ic**	Tóx**ico**	[Quirk # 9]
Umbil**ic**	Umbíl**ico**	
Ur**ic**	Úr**ico**	
Vital**ic**	Vitál**ico**	
Vocal**ic**	Vocál**ico**	
Volcan**ic**	Volcán**ico**	
Xenophob**ic**	Xenofób**ico**	[Quirk # 9 -X pron. like "S]

Exception:

Mast**ic**	Mastíque

There are virtually *hundreds more* words to which this Rule applies, so it's a handy one to remember. Try your hand at translating these:

Don't forget the accent!

Aller**gic**	_____	[One L!]
Microscop**ic**	_____	
Crit**ic**	_____	
Gastr**ic**	_____	
Semant**ic**	_____	

This rule also covers many scientific words:

Chemical Terms [i.e. the names of acids] (ácidos):

Acer**ic**	Acér**ico**	
Acet**ic**	Acét**ico**	
Citr**ic**	Cítr**ico**	
Hydrochlor**ic**	Clorhídr**ico**[3]	[i for y!]
Hydrofluor**ic**	Fluorhídr**ico**[3]	[i for y!]

Lactic	Láctico	
Sulphuric	Sulfúrico	[f for ph!]
Violuric	Violúrico	
Medical Terms :		
Arrhythmic	Arrítmico	[i for y, no TH!]
Hemostatic	Hemostático	[Quirk # 1!]
Hepatic	Hepático	[Quirk # 1!]
Palludic	Palúdico	[only 1 L!]
Spasmodic	Espasmódico	[Quirk # 6!]
Spastic	Espástico	[Quirk # 6!]
Engineering Terms:		
Electronic	Electrónico	
Galvanic	Galvánico	
Metric	Métrico	
Mathematical Terms:		
Algebraic	Algebráico	
Quadratic	Cuadrático	[C for Q!]
Cubic	Cúbico	
Mathematic	Matemático	[no TH!]

and hundreds more that you shouldn't have any trouble thinking of!

---

[1] Interesting word, Arctic; Although in English it is still correct to spell the word with two "c's" (which at one time was also the Spanish spelling: Árctico) the Spanish version has dropped one of the "c's". Strangely, though, the English spelling for "Artichoke" -that delightful cold-climate thistle flower which we eat- is no longer spelled "Arctichoke" (although, until relatively recently, it was). Because most people pronounce the word Arctic as "Artic", it is probably just a matter of time before the spelling is changed. Just a bit of trivia...

[2] You may have noticed that Clinic, Logic, and Republic in Spanish, are Lógica, Clínica and República ! **These are** *feminine-gender* **words!** We will get into that a bit later on in the book...!

[3] As we learned in Chapter One, Spanish is a mirror image of English in that the adjective (modifier) comes *after* the object. In these cases, it is the *hydrogen* that modifies the *fluorine and chlorine,* hence the "switch".

CHAPTER SEVEN

THE ITY RULE
(Major)

This RULE applies to those words in **English** with *more* than two syllables that *end* with the letters

....ity

To translate them into **Spanish**, we will *substitute* the ending with

....idad

As an example, the *English* word Fertili**ty** is the *Spanish* word
Fertil**idad**

Here are some examples:

English		*Spanish*	*Helpful Reminders*
...ity	**=**	**....idad**	
Abili**ty**....................		Abil**idad**	
Agili**ty**....................		Agil**idad**	
Alacri**ty**....................		Alacr**idad**	
Amiabili**ty**...............		Amabil**idad**	[Note diff. in spelling!]
Bestiali**ty**...............		Bestial**idad**	
Banali**ty**..................		Banal**idad**	
Calami**ty**.................		Calam**idad**	
Capaci**ty**.................		Capac**idad**	
Cavi**ty**....................		Cav**idad**	
Compatibili**ty**..........		Compatibil**idad**	
Continui**ty**...............		Continu**idad**	

English	*Spanish*	*Helpful Reminders*
Density	Densidad	
Deity	Deidad	[Diphthong-Pron. ea vowel!]
Ductility	Ductilidad	
Eccentricity	Eccentricidad	[Quirk # 8!]
Elasticity	Elasticidad	
Electricity	Electricidad	
Finality	Finalidad	
Familiarity	Familiaridad	
Frugality	Frugalidad	
Generality	Generalidad	[G pron. like H -Quirk # 12]
Generosity	Generosidad	[G pron. like H -Quirk # 12]
Graduality	Gradualidad	
Hermicity	Hermicidad	[H is silent!]
Horizontality	Horizontalidad	[H is silent!]
Humanity	Humanidad	[H is silent!]
Identity	Identidad	
Immobility	Inmovilidad	[N for M, V for B!]
Impartiality	Imparcialidad	
Instability	Instabilidad	
Intensity	Intensidad	
Justifiability	Justificabilidad	[Quirk # 2!]
Lethality	Letalidad	[T for TH!]
Liability	Liabilidad	
Liberality	Liberalidad	
Luminosity	Luminosidad	
Mediocrity	Mediocridad	
Majority	Mayoridad	[Note diff. Spelling!]
Malignity	Malignidad	
Morbosity	Morbosidad	
Nulity	Nulidad	
Natality	Natalidad	
Neutrality	Neutralidad	
Normality	Normalidad	
Obesity	Obesidad	
Opacity	Opacidad	
Parity	Paridad	
Portability	Portabilidad	

Charles Mazal-Cami

English	Spanish	Helpful Reminders
Punctuality..............	Puntualidad	[Note diff. Spelling!]
Quadruplicity..........	Cuadruplicidad	[c for q!]
Reflectivity.............	Reflectividad	
Salubrity.................	Salubridad	
Sanity.....................	Sanidad	
Sensuality...............	Sensualidad	
Solemnity................	Solemnidad	
Tonality..................	Tonalidad	
Tranquility..............	Tranquilidad	[Quirk # 7]
Ubiquity.................	Ubiquidad	
Unity......................	Unidad	
Vanity....................	Vanidad	
Veracity..................	Veracidad	

Try a few yourself! There are less than four hundred of these, but this
Rule is very accurate (few exceptions).

Senility.................	_____
Radioactivity.........	_____
Inactivity..............	_____
Lubricity..............	_____

Can you *believe* some of the words you know in Spanish?

You really *know* them, too!

Notable exceptions:

English	Spanish	
Antiquity................	Antigüedad	[ü pron. "oo"]
City........................	Ciudad	
Gravity..................	Gravedad	[Note diff. spelling!]
Rarity....................	Rareza	[Note diff. Spelling!]

Also, English words with this ending that have only two syllables, such as
Witty, Bitty, Pity, Gritty etc.

By now you may have discovered that there are many more words "hidden" in these examples. Take one of the previous examples, the English word "Neutrality": by removing the *ending,* you end up with the word "Neutral". In many cases, it works for the Spanish translation as well: remove the ending **...idad** and you have the word "Neutral", which is the proper Spanish translation!

Sensual**ity** without the ending is Sensu**al**; Sensual**idad** without the ending is Sensu**al.** You learned in Chapter Six that English words *ending* in **...al** are the same in Spanish!

Some words such as "Tranquil**ity**" (Tranquil) are *almost* the same in Spanish. "Tranquil", in Spanish, is *"Tranquilo"*; "Solemn**ity**" (Solemn) is "Solemn**idad**" (Solemno)!

CHAPTER EIGHT

THE ISM RULE

(Major)

This Rule applies to those words in **English** that *end* with the letters

....ism

(or ...ysm)

To translate them into **Spanish**, we will *substitute* the ending with

....ismo

As an example, the English word Tour**ism** is the Spanish word Tur**ismo**

In this example, you will have noticed the difference in Spelling.
You will recall that in Chapter One we established that

Spanish is pronounced exactly as it is written!

The English word TOURISM is pronounced *TOO*-RISM, with the "U"
being silent (that is, not participating in the pronunciation of the word).

The Spanish word, TURISMO, is pronounced *TOO*-REES-MO.
If the spelling had included the "OU", it would have been
TOH-OOR-EES-MO.   Not good!

English is phonetic (which, as you learned in Chapter Six, is "fonético") meaning that words are spelled according to their *sound*. Spanish, on the other hand, is pronounced according to the *spelling*, and no "trick combinations" of letters are allowed!

In Spanish, if you can pronounce the word, you can spell it and vice-versa.

How is *that* for easy?

Anyway, here are a few more examples:

English	*Spanish*	*Helpful Reminders*
....ism/ysm =	**....ismo**	
Ab**ysm**..................	Ab**ísmo***	[I for Y!]
Anachron**ism**..........	Anacron**ísmo**	[C for CH!]
Babt**ism**..................	Baut**ísmo**	[Note diff.Spelling]
Cauter**ism**..............	Cauter**ísmo**	
Cannibal**ism**...........	Canibal**ísmo**	[Only one N!]
Colloquial**ism**..........	Coloquial**ísmo**	[Only 1 L!]
Darwin**ism**..............	Darwin**ísmo**	
Dynam**ism**..............	Dinam**ísmo**	[I for Y!]
Embol**ism**..............	Embol**ísmo**	
Euphon**ism**..............	Eufon**ísmo**	[Quirk # 5!]
Fanatic**ism**..............	Fanatic**ísmo**	[Quirk # 8]
Geotrop**ism**..............	Geotrop**ísmo**	
Heliotrop**ism**...........	Heliotrop**ísmo**	[H is Silent!]
Herbal**ism**..............	Herbal**ísmo**	[H is Silent!]
Imag**ism**..................	Imag**ísmo**	
Imperial**ism**.............	Imperial**ísmo**	
Impression**ism**.........	Impresion**ísmo**	[Only 1 S!]
Legal**ism**..................	Legal**ísmo**	
Martial**ism**..............	Marcial**ísmo**	[Note C for T!]
Material**ism**.............	Material**ísmo**	
Mystic**ism**..............	Mistic**ísmo**	[Note I for Y!]
Novel**ism**..............	Novel**ísmo**	
Occult**ism**..............	Ocult**ísmo**	[Only 1 C!]
Opportun**ism**...........	Oportun**ísmo**	[Only 1 P!]
Prism......................	Pr**ísma****	[Feminine Gender!]
Paternal**ism**.............	Paternal**ísmo**	

English	_Spanish_	_Helpful Reminders_
Phototrop**ism**............	Fototrop**ísmo**	[Quirk # 5!]
Quiet**ism**.................	Quiet**ísmo**	[Quirk #7!]
Rational**ism**............	Racional**ísmo**	[Note C for T!]
Real**ism**..................	Real**ísmo**	
Ritual**ism**................	Ritual**ísmo**	
Sad**ism**...................	Sad**ísmo**	
Social**ism**................	Social**ísmo**	
Totalitarian**ism**	Tolitarian**ísmo**	
Universal**ism**............	Universal**ísmo**	
Utalitarian**ism**...........	Utalitarian**ísmo**	
Volcan**ism**................	Volcan**ísmo**	

You may be surprised to learn that there are nearly three-hundred *other* ISM's in English! Many of them, however, are derived from Greek-root words that most of us have never heard of. But look at it this way: A few moments ago, who would have *ever* thought that you would know the Spanish translation for the word **Transcendentalism?!**

To prove a point, translate the following examples:
(Don't forget the accent!)

Aneur**ism**.................   _____

Individual**ism** ....   _____

Mercantil**ism**............   _____

Organ**ism**.................   _____

Sensual**ism**..............   _____

*The English word, Abysm, is not as commonly used (in English) as Abyss; however, in Spanish, "Abismo" is a rather common word. Latin America is very mountainous and, consequently, is full of "Abismos".

**Oops! Another pesky *feminine gendered* word! Be patient. We'll get to that..!

There are approximately 200,000 English words catalogued in most unabridged English-language dictionaries. These do not include many more thousands of specialized terms, slang words of common usage, professional verbage and foreign words that have been "incorporated" into popular English. The total number of words used in the English language is phenomenal. It isn't surprising, then, to learn that at least 75,000 words in English are rooted in commonspace with Spanish! There are words in English, particularly technical terminology, that have no similar counterparts in Spanish. The Spanish language academies have been slow to assimilate new words into the language, so words such as"OK", "grid", "quark", "chip", "modem", and "stunt" , among many others, have no *precise* Spanish translation. English, on the other hand, borrows words from other languages quite readily. Many aeronautical terms, like "aileron" and "fuselage" were simply taken from French and incorporated, for lack of an *English* description. English includes many Spanish words, such as "taco", "adios", "villa", and "corral" all of which are of common, popular usage, and are in the dictionary. Spanish, on the the other hand, popularly *uses* many English words, although they have not yet been assimilated by the academicians. Words like "O.K." *(Sp. "oquei),* T-Bone *(Sp. "tibón"),* Motel *(Sp. "motel"),* Sandwich *(Sp. Sanwich),* Football *(Sp. Futbol)* and Baseball *(Sp. Beisbol)* are commonly used throughout Latin America, but not one of them has made it into the Spanish dictionaries! This gives much meaning to the words of J. Vendryes! [see Page 10]

Charles Mazal-Cami

CHAPTER NINE

THE **SION** RULE

(Major)

This Rule applies to those words in **English** that *end* with the letters

....sion

To translate them into **Spanish**, we will *substitute* the ending with

...sión

?

What's this?

This ought to be *very* easy!

It is! **We write them exactly as they are in English!**

Well, not *exactly*: <u>remember the Quirks!</u>
Also, no double letters (GG, MM, NN, PP, SS or TT)
and F instead of PH.

For example, the English word Compul<u>sion</u> is the **same** in Spanish
except that we accentuate the last syllable (it ends in "..ión")
[see "Accents", Chapter One]

Here are some examples:

English		_Spanish_	[Helpful Reminders]
....sion	=	....sión	
Aspersion...............		Aspersión	
Compassion.............		Compasión	[only 1 S]
Comprehension		Comprehensión	[H is Silent!]
Compulsion.............		Compulsión	
Conclusion.............		Conclusión	
Confusion...............		Confusión	
Decision.................		Decisión	
Defusion................		Defusión	
Fission...................		Fisión	[Only 1 S!]
Fusion...................		Fusión	
Illusion.................		Ilusión	[Only 1 L!]
Lesion....................		Lesión	
Mission.................		Misión	[Only 1 S!]
Passion.................		Pasion	[Only 1 S!]
Pension.................		Pensión	
Seclusion...............		Seclusión	
Session.................		Sesión	[Only 1 S!]
Tension.................		Tensión	

Well, anyway, you get the idea.

We can skip the practice se**ssion**.
(You *already* know how to write in English!)

Unfortunately, there aren't *that* many words in this Rule.
Somewhat less than three hundred, perhaps.
But it counts; after all, it *is* Spanish!

CHAPTER TEN

THE OUS RULE
(Major)

This Rule applies to those words in **English** that *end* with the letters

....ous
(Except those preceded by "ti")

To translate them into **Spanish,** we will *substitute* the ending with

....oso

As an example, the **English** word Gase<u>ous</u> is the Spanish word Gase<u>oso</u>.

(Remember to pronounce all the Spanish vowels!)
Here are some additional words:

English	*Spanish*	*Helpful Reminders*
....ous =	**....oso**	
Adventur<u>ous</u>............	Aventur<u>oso</u>	[Note diff. Spelling!]
Amor**ous**.................	Amor**oso**	
Asper**ous**................	Asper**oso**	
Auspicious..............	Auspicioso	
Avaricious...............	Avaricioso	
Billious.................	Bilioso	[Only one L!]
Bulb**ous**................	Bulb**oso**	

English	Spanish	Helpful Reminders
Cadaverous.............	Cadaveroso	
Callous..................	Calloso	[Pron. CA-YO-SO!]
Capacious...............	Capacioso	
Capcious................	Capcioso	
Curious..................	Curioso	
Deciduous.............	Deciduoso	
Delicious...............	Delicioso	
Estrous..................	Estroso	
Factuous................	Factuoso	
Fallacious..............	Falacioso	[Note 1 L!]
Fastidious..............	Fastidioso	
Fibromatous............	Fibromatoso	
Fibrous..................	Fibroso	
Generous...............	Generoso	[Quirk # 12]
Glacious................	Glacioso	
Glamorous.............	Glamoroso	
Glorious................	Glorioso	
Gracious................	Gracioso	[in Sp. Means "funny"]
Harmonious............	Harmonioso	[H is Silent!]
Imperious..............	Imperioso	
Laborious..............	Laborioso	
Leprous.................	Leproso	
Luminous...............	Luminoso	
Malodorous............	Malodoroso	
Monstrous..............	Monstruoso	[Note incl. of "U"]
Melodious..............	Melodioso	
Nitrous..................	Nitroso	
Pompous................	Pomposo	
Porous..................	Poroso	
Pretencious............	Pretencioso	
Querulous..............	Queruloso	[Quirk # 7!]
Repeticious............	Repeticioso	
Rigorous................	Rigoroso	
Scandalous.............	Escandaloso	[Quirk # 6!]
Spacious................	Espacioso	[Quirk # 6]
Sulphurous.............	Sulfuroso	[Quirk # 5!]
Tendencious............	Tendencioso	

English	Spanish	Helpful Reminders
Tortu**ous**...............	Tortu**oso**	
Tremul**ous**.............	Tremul**oso**	
Vapor**ous**..............	Vapor**oso**	
Vici**ous**...................	Vici**oso**	
Virtu**ous**.................	Virtu**oso**	
Virul**ous**.................	Virul**oso**	

OK. Now *you* fill in the blanks!

Albumin**ous**............	_____	
Fastu**ous**.................	_____	
Mellodi**ous**............	_____	[Note one L!]
Preci**ous**.................	_____	
Religi**ous**................	_____	
Glutin**ous**..............	_____	

Some exceptions:

English	Spanish
Capricious	Caprichoso
Ferocious	Feroz
Odorous	Oloroso
Pious	Piedadoso
Temptacious	Tentacioso
Tenacious	Tenaz
Tremendous	Tremendo
Voracious	Voraz

English words ending in

....*ti*ous

can be translated to **Spanish** by *substituting* the ending with

....*ci*oso

As an example, the **English** word ambi**tious** is the
Spanish word ambi**cioso**

The English endings ...tious and ...cious
both *sound* the same.
They both have an "S" sound.English can be very complicated.
Perhaps the real complexity in learning Spanish is understanding how to
uncomplicate English!

In Chapter One we learned that double consonants are not used in
Spanish, with the exception of the C and the R.

Also, we have seen that Spanish does not have tricky letter combinations
like KN, or PH!

Here is a reminder of what *isn't* allowed in Spanish

In **Spanish**, we have learned, the **"T"** always *sounds* like a **"T"**, which
is true for *all* of the consonants. Each letter *sounds* like what it is!

Inasmuch as the **....tious** in English *sounds* like an "S", the Spanish
translation (**...ci**oso) keeps it that way!

English	Spanish
AE..............	E
BB..............	B
CZ..............	Z
DD............	D
FF..............	F
GG............	G
KN..............	no words
LL..............	L
MM............	M
NN..............	N
PP..............	P
PF..............	F
PH..............	F
SS..............	S
TT..............	T

CHAPTER ELEVEN

THE ENT RULE

(Major)

This Rule applies to those words in **English** that *end* in

....ent

*(Except ....me*nt)*

To translate them into **Spanish**, we will *substitute* the ending with:

....ente

Thus, the English word Accid**ent** is the
Spanish word Accid**ente**

Some more examples:

English		*Spanish*	*Helpful Reminders*
....ent	=	**....ente**	
Afflu**ent**.............		Aflu**ente**	[Only 1 F!]
Appar**ent**............		Aparente	[Only 1 P!]
Astring**ent**..........		Astringente	[Quirk # 12]
Cli**ent**...............		Cliente	
Coeffici**ent**........		Coefici**ente**	[Only 1 F!]

English	Spanish	Helpful Reminders
Coincident.........	Coincidente	
Consistent..........	Consistente	
Continent..........	Continente	
Decent..............	Decente	
Detergent...........	Detergente	
Different...........	Diferente	[Only 1 F!]
Efficient............	Eficiente	[Only 1 F!]
Eminent..............	Eminente	
Equivalent..........	Equivalente	[Quirk # 7!]
Excellent...........	Excelente	[Only 1 L!]
Existent..............	Existente	
Fluorescent.........	Fluorescente	
Gradient.............	Gradiente	
Impudent...........	Impudente	
Inconvenient.......	Inconveniente	
Indifferent..........	Indiferente	[Only 1 F!]
Innocent.............	Inocente	[Only 1 N!]
Insurgent...........	Insurgente	
Intelligent...........	Inteligente	[Only 1 L!]
Intermitent..........	Intermitente	
Latent.................	Latente	
Malevolent.........	Malevolente	
Micronutrient......	Micronutriente	
Nutrient..............	Nutriente	
Obedient............	Obediente	
Occident.............	Occidente	
Omnipotent.........	Omnipotente	
Opulent..............	Opulente	
Orient................	Oriente	
Pacient..............	Paciente	
Permanent..........	Permanente	
President............	Presidente	
Propellent...........	Propelente	[Only 1 L!]
Proponent...........	Proponente	
Prudent..............	Prudente	
Recurrent...........	Recurrente	
Repellent...........	Repelente	[Only 1 L!]

English	Spanish	Helpful Reminders
Rent..................	**Renta**	[Omigosh! Another femenine gender!]
Resolv**ent**..........	Resolv**ente**	
Revolv**ent**.........	Revolv**ente**	
Resurg**ent**..........	Resurg**ente**	
Sali**ent**...............	Sali**ente**	[also Sobresaliente]
Solv**ent**..............	Solv**ente**	
Suffici**ent**...........	Sufici**ente**	[Only 1 F!]
Transpar**ent**........	Transpar**ente**	
Urg**ent**...............	Urg**ente**	
Vice-Presid**ent**...	Vice-Presid**ente**	

Try a few yourself!:

Delincu**ent**.........	_____
Indol**ent**.............	_____
Pat**ent**................	_____
Resid**ent**............	_____

Exceptions:

Content (happy)....	Contento	
Content [volume]...	Contenido	
Event................	Evento	
Purulent............	Purulento	
Serpent............	Serpiente	
Succulent.........	Suculento	[Only 1 C!]
Turbulent..........	Turbulento	
Unguent............	Ungüento	[Notice the ü! Pron. "oo"]
Violent..............	Violento	

To translate **English** words that end in

....*m*ent,

we will *substitute* the ending with

....mento

The **English** word Mo**ment**
is the **Spanish** word Mo**mento**

Additional examples of **....ment** are:

English		*Spanish*	*Helpful Reminders*
....ment	=	**....mento**	
Apart**ment**..........		Aparta**mento**	[Add an A!]
Argu**ment**...........		Argu**mento**	
Arma**ment**..........		Arma**mento**	
Cement..............		**Cemento**	
Compart**ment**......		Comparti**mento**	[Add an I!]
Depart**ment**........		Departa**mento**	[Add an A!]
Fo**ment**..............		Fo**mento**	
Impedi**ment**........		Impedi**mento**	
Sedi**ment**...........		Sedi**mento**	
Segment...........		**Segmento**	

Some exceptions:

Com**ment**...........	Comentario	
Derail**ment**........	Desrielado	
Establish**ment**....	Establecimiento	
Judge**ment**.........	Juicio	
Senti**ment**..........	Sentimiento	[Add an I!]

Let's **pause** for a moment!

Are you a *believer* yet?

Ask yourself, how many Spanish
words did you KNOW before you opened this book?

Since we are at least a few minutes ahead of schedule,
TAKE A TWO-MINUTE BREAK!

CHAPTER TWELVE

THE **ALLY** RULE
(Major)

This Rule is just a bit tricky, so read on carefully!

This Rule applies to those words in **English** that *end* with the letters

....ally

To translate them into **Spanish**, we will *substitute the <u>last two letters</u>* of the **English** ending (**...al*ly***) with

....mente

Thus, the English word casual*ly* is the Spanish word casual**mente**

<u>However</u> (here's the kicker), *if the English word ends in* ....<u>c</u>**ally**
(as in Automati<u>c</u>**ally**)
we keep the "**c**" and *substitute* ....**ally** with ....<u>a</u>mente
and the Spanish translation becomes Automatic**<u>amente</u>**

It is grammatically correct to use accents on these words (as shown in the following examples), although "modern" Spanish has become "lazy" about using them. In keeping with the times, you can also
forget the accent
(We've put it there to remind you where the stress should be).

Here are some more examples:

English		Spanish	Helpful Reminders
ally	=	**....mente**	
cally	=	**....amente**	

English	Spanish	Helpful Reminders
Artifici**ally**..............	Artificial**ménte**	
Anatomi**cally**.........	Anatomic**aménte**	
Benefici**ally**............	Beneficial**ménte**	
Bilater**ally**...............	Bilateral**ménte**	
Casu**ally**.................	Casual**ménte**	
Categori**cally**.........	Categoric**aménte**	
Decim**ally**...............	Decimal**ménte**	
Democrati**cally**......	Democratic**aménte**	
Emotion**ally**............	Emocional**ménte**	[Note C for T]
Economi**cally**.........	Economic**aménte**	
Especi**ally**...............	Especial**ménte**	
Faci**ally**...................	Facial**ménte**	
Fanati**cally**.............	Fanatic**aménte**	
Geneti**cally**.............	Genetic**aménte**	[Quirk # 12]
Generi**cally**.............	Generic**aménte**	[Quirk # 12]
Hermeti**cally**...........	Hermetic**aménte**	[H is silent!]
Hereti**cally**..............	Heretic**aménte**	[H is silent!]
Intrinsi**cally**...........	Intrinsic**aménte**	
Ironi**cally**...............	Ironic**aménte**	
Later**ally**.................	Lateral**ménte**	
Legitim**ally**.............	Legitima**ménte**	[slightly diff. spell.!]
Logi**cally**...............	Logic**aménte**	[slightly diff. spell.!]
Mechani**cally**.........	Mecanic**aménte**	[Quirk # 8]
Methodi**cally**.........	Metodic**aménte**	[Note no H!]
Numeri**cally**............	Numeric**aménte**	
Offici**ally**................	Oficial**ménte**	
Neurologi**cally**.......	Neurologic**aménte**	[Only 1 F!]
Opti**cally**................	Optic**aménte**	
Pacifi**cally**..............	Pacific**aménte**	
Parci**ally**................	Parcial**ménte**	

English	*Spanish*	*Helpful Reminders*
Racia***lly***...............	Racial**ménte**	
Rationa***lly***.............	Racional**ménte**	[Note C for T]
Sensua***lly***..............	Sensual**ménte**	
Socia***lly***...............	Social**ménte**	
Specia***lly***.............	Especial**ménte**	[Quirk # 6!]
Topica***lly***.............	Topica**ménte**	
Tota***lly***.................	Total**ménte**	
Umbilica***lly***...........	Umbilica**ménte**	
Universa***lly***...........	Universal**ménte**	
Vagina***lly***..............	Vaginal**ménte**	
Virtua***lly***..............	Virtual**ménte**	

Practice on a few yourself!

Classic***ally***...........	_____	[Note one S!]
Hexagon***ally***........	_____	[H is silent!]
Individu***ally***.........	_____	
Initi***ally***..............	_____	["C" for "T"]
Medicin***ally***.........	_____	
Periodic***ally***.........	_____	
Radic***ally***.............	_____	
Specific***ally***.........	_____	[Quirk # 6!]

You might take into account that there are many other words in English that *end* in ...ly. The above Rule takes into consideration only those that end in ...**al**ly because *there are very few exceptions to this Rule.*

English words ending in **....ly** (other than **....ally**) can be translated to Spanish simply by *preceding* the **....mente** ending with either an "**a**", or an "**e**", thus: **....amente** or **....emente**. But there *are* some exceptions (in other words, it doesn't *always* "work out").

There are English words ending with
....bly (Terrib*ly*)	*Sp.* Terribl**eménte**
....dly (Candid*ly*)	*Sp.* Candida**ménte**
....tly (Correct*ly*)	*Sp.* Correcta**ménte**

where substituting with …amente and …emente *usually* works out fine.

The spelling of the word in the Spanish translation will sometimes *vary* a bit, but it will be close enough to be understood.
Here are some examples:

English	*Spanish*	*Reminders & Notes*
Appreciab**ly**.........	Apreciabl**eménte**	[Only 1 P!]
Candi**dly**............	Candid**aménte**	
Cal**mly**...............	Calmad**aménte**	[It's Close!]
Correc**tly**...........	Correct**aménte**	
Elegant**ly**...........	Elegant**eménte**	
Eloquent**ly**..........	Elocuent**eménte**	[C for Q!]
Fabulous**ly**..........	Fabulos**aménte**	[It's Close!]
Fervent**ly**...........	Fervent**eménte**	
Magnificent**ly**.....	Magnific**aménte**	
Notab**ly**..............	Notabl**eménte**	
Necessari**lly**........	Necesari**aménte**	[Only 1 S!]
Oppulent**ly**..........	Opulent**aménte**	[Only 1 P!]
Patient**ly**............	Pacient**eménte**	[C for T!]
Perfect**ly**............	Perfect**aménte**	
Terri**bly**.............	Terribl**eménte**	
Variab**ly**.............	Variabl**eménte**	
Violent**ly**............	Violent**aménte**	

Whew! Well, *that's as tough as it gets!*
If you managed to get through *this* Rule unscathed, you might also try your hand at learning Venecian and Basque.
(And don't worry, you'll know the alloted number of words even *without* this Rule!)

CHAPTER THIRTEEN

THE **ARY** RULE
ORY

(Major)

This is a Double Rule!

This Rule applies to those words in **English** that *end* with the letters

....ary

OR

....ory

To translate them into **Spanish**,

we will *substitute* the English ending ....ary with **....ario**

and we will *substitute* the English ending ....ory with **....orio**

Thus, the **English** word ordin**ary** is the **Spanish** word ordin**ario**
And the **English** word acces**ory** is the **Spanish** word acces**orio**.

Some further [mixed] examples of these are:

English		*Spanish*	*Helpful Reminders*
....ary	=	....ario	
....ory	=	....orio	

English	Spanish	Helpful Reminders
Accusat**ory**	Acusat**orio**	[Only 1 C!]
Advers**ary**	Advers**ario**	
Annivers**ary**	Anivers**ario**	[Only 1 N!]
Appelat**ory**	Apelat**orio**	[Note 1 P!]
Benedict**ory**	Benedict**orio**	
Can**ary**	Can**ario**	
Categ**ory**	Categor**ia**	[Femenine Gender!]*
Castigat**ory**	Castigat**orio**	
Centen**ary**	Centen**ario**	
Compensat**ory**	Compensat**orio**	
Conciliat**ory**	Conciliat**orio**	
Conservat**ory**	Conservat**orio**	
Cremat**ory**	Cremat**orio**	
Culin**ary**	Culin**ario**	
Declamat**ory**	Declamat**orio**	
Defamat**ory**	Defamat**orio**	
Derogat**ory**	Derogat**orio**	
Direct**ory**	Direct**orio**	
Element**ary**	Element**ario**	[Also Elemental]
Eliminat**ory**	Eliminat**orio**	
Emasculat**ory**	Emasculat**orio**	
Exculpat**ory**	Exculpat**orio**	
Explorat**ory**	Explorat**orio**	
Fact**ory**	Factor**ia**	[See Note Below!]**
Fulminat**ory**	Fulminat**orio**	
Gesticulat**ory**	Gesticulat**orio**	[Quirk # 12]
Gl**ory**	Glor**ia**	[Feminine Gender!]*
Hist**ory**	Histor**ia**	[Feminine Gender!]*
Illus**ory**	Ilus**orio**	[Note 1 L!]

Charles Mazal-Cami

English	Spanish	Helpful Reminders
Inflammatory	Inflamatorio	[Only 1 M!]
Lavatory	Lavatorio	
Laboratory	Laboratorio	
Mammary	Mamario	[Note 1 M!]
Mandatory	Mandatorio	
Maxillary	Maxilario	[Note 1 L!]
Moratory***	Moratorio	
Notary	Notario	
Observatory	Observatorio	
Octogenary	Octogenario	
Olfactory	Olfactorio	
Offertory	Ofertorio	[Note 1 F!]
Ordinary	Ordinario	
Parliamentary	Parlamentario	[Note diff. Sp.!]
Plagiary	Plagiario	
Penitenciary	Penitenciaria	[Feminine Gender!]*
Postulatory	Postulatorio	
Predatory	Predatorio	
Proprietary	Propietario	[Note diff. Sp.!]
Pulsatory	Pulsatorio	
Questionary	Cuestionario	[Note C for Q!]
Refectory	Refectorio	
Refractory	Refractario	[Note diff. Sp.!]
Regulatory	Regulatorio	
Respiratory	Respiratorio	
Retaliatory	Retaliatorio	
Salutatory	Salutatorio	
Secretary	Secretario	
Sensory	Sensorio	
Solitary	Solitario	
Speculatory	Especulatorio	[Quirk # 6!]
Summary	Sumario	[Only 1 M!]
Supervisory	Supervisorio	
Temporary	Temporario	
Terminatory	Terminatorio	

Although there are perhaps *less* than three hundred words in English with these endings, this Rule is extremely accurate. There are *very* few exceptions. These are some relevant ones:

Savory........................... Sabroso
Armory........................ Armeria
Story........................... Cuento
Gory........................... Aparatoso
Glory........................... Gloria

There might be a *few* others...

Anyway, if you've been attentive to this *Double Rule*, you should not have any problem translating a few words on your own!
Try these:

Ambulat**ory**............ _____
Confiscat**ory**........... _____
Contr**ary**................ _____
Dormit**ory**.............. _____
Obligat**ory**............. _____
Pulmon**ary**............. _____
Purgat**ory**.............. _____
Subsidi**ary**............. _____

Doesn't it feel *wonderful* to be writing in a "foreign" language?!

---

*You may have noticed that more of those *femenine gender* words creeped in - we *must* to clear that up! Chapter Eighteen might help, if you are in a hurry. Otherwise, just read on with the rest of us!

** The word FACT<u>ORY</u> is translated above to Spanish as FACT<u>ORIA</u>. This word, although correct, is rarely used. The modern usage would be FABRICA, a place where things are *fabricated!* (We've learned that FABRIC<u>ATE</u> translates to FABRIC<u>AR</u> [Chapter Three]. In English, of course, *Fabricate* means to *manufacture*, or *make*, something.

***Morator<u>ium</u> is *also* Moratorio in Spanish.

CHAPTER FOURTEEN

THE **BLE** RULE
(Major)

This is a very *interesting* Rule
(You are going to love it!)

....ble

Words in **English** that have this ending are *exactly the same*
in **Spanish!**

There *are* exceptions, some of which we will list further on, but you will
find that the very large majority of words in **English** ending in ...ble are
identical in meaning and spelling when translated to **Spanish**.

You must, of course, observe the Quirks in Chapter One.

Here are some examples:

English		*Spanish*	*Helpful Reminders*
....ble	=	**....ble**	
Admissi**ble**...............		Admisi**ble**	[Only 1 S!]
Aliena**ble**................		Aliena**ble**	
Applica**ble**...............		Aplica**ble**	[Only 1 P!]
Cable......................		**Cable**	
Calcula**ble**...............		Calcula**ble**	
Compara**ble**............		Compara**ble**	
Compati**ble**.............		Compati**ble**	
Comprehensi**ble**.......		Comprehensi**ble**	[Quirk # 1]
Considera**ble**...........		Considera**ble**	
Consola**ble**.............		Consola**ble**	
Corrigi**ble**...............		Corregi**ble**	[E for I!]

English	Spanish	Helpful Reminders
Corruptible............	Corruptible	
Curable................	Curable	
Delible................	Delible	
Depreciable...........	Depreciable	
Dirigible..............	Dirigible	
Destructible..........	Destructible	
Determinable..........	Determinable	
Divisible..............	Divisible	
Durable................	Durable	
Executable............	Executable*	[X is pronounced like Eng. H]
Explicable............	Explicable*	[X is pron. like Eng. X]
Exportable............	Exportable	
Fallible..............	Falible	[Only 1 L!]
Flammable.............	Flamable	[Only 1 M!]
Flexible..............	Flexible*	[X is pronounced like X]
Horrible..............	Horrible	[Quirk # 1!]
Hospitable............	Hospitable	[Quirk # 1!]
Immitable.............	Imitable	[Only 1 M!]
Implacable............	Implacable	
Impossible............	Imposible	[Only 1 S!]
Impregnable...........	Impregnable	
Imputable.............	Imputable	
Incessable............	Incesable	[Only 1 S!]
Indelible.............	Indelible	
Indispensable.........	Indispensable	
Indivisible...........	Indivisible	
Indomitable...........	Indomitable	
Inflammable...........	Inflamable	[Only 1 M!]
Innumerable...........	Innumerable	
Irrefutable...........	Irrefutable	[Practice rolling your Rs!]
Irrevocable...........	Irrevocable	[Ditto...]
Irrisistible..........	Irrisistible	[Ditto...]
Lamentable............	Lamentable	
Laudible..............	Laudible	
Malleable.............	Maleable	[Only 1 L!]
Memorable.............	Memorable	
Moldable..............	Moldeable	[Add an E!]

Charles Mazal-Cami

English	Spanish	Helpful Reminders
Mutable...............	Mutable	
Narrable...............	Narrable	
Navegable.............	Navegable	
Notable.................	Notable	
Objectionable.........	Objecionable	[No T!]
Observable.............	Observable	
Omissible...............	Omisible	[Only 1 S!]
Operable...............	Operable	
Passable.................	Pasable	[Only 1 S!]
Permeable.............	Permeable	
Permissible.............	Permisible	[Only 1 S!]
Portable.................	Portable	
Possible.................	Posible	[Only 1 S!]
Practicable.............	Practicable	
Probable.................	Probable	
Reducible...............	Reducible	
Refutable.................	Refutable	
Removable.............	Removible	[I for A!]
Reversible...............	Reversible	
Sable.....................	Sable	
Sensible.................	Sensible	
Sociable.................	Sociable	
Supportable.............	Soportable	[Only 1 P!]
Terminable.............	Terminable	
Terrible.................	Terrible	
Traversable.............	Traversible	[I for A!]
Useable.................	Usable	[drop an E!]
Violable.................	Violable	
Vulnerable.............	Vulnerable	

* [See Quirk # 9]

Go ahead and admit it: that was fun!
Who said Spanish was a *foreign* language?

This Rule is accurate approximately 80% of the time, and there are many, many hundreds of words to which this Rule *does* apply.

There are many additional words in English with this ending that use the Prefixes "in.." or "im.." (i.e., **In**calcula**ble**, **Im**penetra**ble**, **In**compati**ble**, **In**hospita**ble**, etc.);   these are *also* identical in Spanish.

One of the peculiarities of the English language is that we tend to *invent* words rather frequently that more closely express our thoughts. The *suffix* "....A<u>BLE</u>" is no exception, either. This suffix implies the ability to perform the action of the verb to which it is attached.

For example, if we feel that it is possible to jump over a specific wall, we might describe that wall as being "jumpA<u>BLE</u>", even if the word is not to be found in any dictionary!

If you want to recognize many of the words for which the **...ble** Rule does <u>NOT</u> apply, those would be **English** words that can be preceded by the *Prefix* **"un"** (i.e. **un**predicta**ble**, **un**recognizea**ble**, **un**moveable, etc.). The **Spanish** Prefix **"in.."** is *substituted* for **"un.."**), as shown below in brackets.

These are some of the more salient words for which this rule *does NOT* apply:

English		*Spanish*
[Un]able	....	[In]capáz
[Un]believable	....	[In]creible
Bible	....	Biblia
[In]capable	....	[In]capáz
Edible	....	Comestible
Fable	....	Cuento
[Un]manageable	....	[In]manejable
Mandible	....	Mandíbula
Marble (the rock)	....	Marmol
Marble (the toy)	....	Canica
[Un]measurable	....	[In]medible
[Un]moveable	....	[In]movible
[Un]obtainable	....	[In]obtenible
Predictable	....	Predecible
Reconizeable	....	Reconozible
[Un]sustainable	....	[In]sostenible
Syllable	....	Sílaba
Table (to sit at)	....	Mesa
Table (a listing)	....	Tabla
[Un]predictable	....	Impredicible (also Imprevisto)
[Un]thinkable	....	[In]pensable
[Un]translatable	....	[In]traducible
Trouble	....	Dificultad
Unrecognizeable	....	Irreconozible

CHAPTER FIFTEEN

THE **IVE** RULE
(Major)

This Rule applies to those words in **English** with *two or more syllables*
that *end* with the letters

...ive

To translate those words into Spanish
we will *substitute* the English ending with

...ivo
[pronounced <u>EE</u>-VO]

Thus, the *English* word instructive is the *Spanish* word instructivo

The next-to-last syllable (the "i") receives *stress* [see "Accents" Rule I, Page 6]

This is our last Chapter covering the Major Rules!
There is *much more* in the chapters ahead, but at this point you have
learned more than
twenty thousand words in Spanish!

As an encouragement, and to show you what *just this single Rule* will
teach you, we will set forth *many* more examples than in the previous
Chapters. This will give you a visual idea of how much Spanish you have
actually learned!

English		Spanish	Helpful Reminders
....ive	=	....ivo	
Abortive......................		Abortivo	
Abrasive......................		Abrasivo	
Abrogative..................		Abrogativo	
Absorptive...................		Absorptivo	
Abstersive..................		Adsertivo	[D for B!]
Abstractive..................		Abstractivo	
Abusive.......................		Abusivo	
Active.........................		Activo	
Adaptive......................		Adaptivo	
Additive......................		Aditivo	[Note 1 D!]
Adhesive.....................		Adhesivo	[Quirk # 1!]
Adictive......................		Adictivo	
Adjective.....................		Adjetivo	[No C!]
Adoptive......................		Adoptivo	
Adsorptive..................		Adsorptivo	
Affirmative.................		Afirmativo	[Only 1 F!]
Agressive....................		Agresivo	[Only 1 S!]
Assimilative.................		Asimilativo	[Only 1 S!]
Attractive...................		Atractivo	[Only 1 T!]
Benedictive.................		Benedictivo	
Calculative.................		Calculativo	
Capacitive..................		Capacitivo	
Circumspective............		Circunspectivo	[N for M!]
Cohesive.....................		Cohesivo	
Collective...................		Colectivo	[Only 1 L!]
Comparative................		Comparativo	
Comprehensive............		Comprehensivo	[Quirk # 1!]
Conclusive...................		Conclusivo	
Confirmative...............		Confirmativo	
Consecutive................		Consecutivo	
Conservative...............		Conservativo	[also Conservador]
Contraceptive..............		Contraceptivo	
Cooperative................		Cooperativo	
Corroborative..............		Corroborativo	
Creative......................		Creativo	
Cumulative..................		Cumulativo	[also Acumulativo]
Defective....................		Defectivo	
Defensive...................		Defensivo	
Definitive....................		Definitivo	
Demonstrative.............		Demostrativo	[No N!]
Derogative..................		Derogativo	
Destructive.................		Destructivo	

English	Spanish	Helpful Reminders
Diges<u>tive</u>	Diges<u>tivo</u>	
Diminutive	Diminutivo	
Directive	Directivo	
Distinctive	Distinctivo	
Effective	Efectivo	[Only 1 F!]
Effusive	Efusivo	[Only 1 F!]
Excessive	Excesivo	[Note 1 S!]
Exclusive	Exclusivo	
Executive	Ejecutivo	[Note J for X! Quirk # 2!]
Expletive	Expletivo	[Quirk # 9]
Explosive	Explosivo	[Quirk # 9]
Extensive	Extensivo	[Quirk # 9]
Festive	Festivo	
Figurative	Figurativo	
Formative	Formativo	
Fugitive	Fugitivo	
Furtive	Furtivo	
Gesticulative	Gesticulativo	
Gramnegative	Gramnegativo	
Grampositive	Grampositivo	
Gravitative	Gravitativo	
Gustative	Gustativo	
Hydropositive	Hidrypositivo	[Note I for Y!]
Hypersensitive	Hipersensitivo	[Note I for Y!]
Hypertensive	Hipertensivo	[Note I for Y!]
Illustrative	Ilustrativo	[Note 1 L!]
Imperative	Imperativo	
Incentive	Incentivo	
Initiative	Initiative	
Inovative	Inovativo	
Intensive	Intensivo	
Inquisitive	Inquisitivo	
Instinctive	Instinctivo	
Instructive	Instructivo	
Invasive	Invasivo	
Judicative	Judicativo	
Justificative	Justificativo	
Lacerative	Lacerativo	
Laxative	Laxativo	
Legislative	Legislativo	
Locomotive	Locomotivo	[the adverb]
Locomotive	Locomo<u>tora</u>	[the noun]
Memorative	Memorativo	
Missive	Misivo	[Only 1 S!]
Molestive	Molestivo	

English	Spanish	Helpful Reminders
Native............................	Nativo	
Negative........................	Negativo	
Obstructive...................	Obstructivo	
Offensive.......................	Ofensivo	[Only 1 F!]
Operative.......................	Operativo	
Pensive..........................	Pensivo	
Positive.........................	Positivo	
Preservative..................	Preservativo	
Reactive........................	Reactivo	
Receptive......................	Receptivo	
Respective.....................	Respectivo	
Responsive....................	Responsivo	
Secretive.......................	Secretivo	
Seductive......................	Seductivo	
Selective.......................	Selectivo	
Significative..................	Significativo	
Subversive....................	Subversivo	
Suggestive....................	Sugestivo	[Only 1 G!]
Superlative...................	Superlativo	
Tentative......................	Tentativo	

Well, pretty descrip<u>tive</u> (descrip<u>tivo</u>), yes?

Notable exceptions:

Impressive....................	Impresionante	
Locomotive [the noun]......	Locomotora	

What?

You want *more?*

OK, *OK!* Because this is the last of the Major Rules, we'll get into *more* detail. This will give you an even *better* idea of how many words in Spanish you have just learned.

(You *might* even learn a few more words in *English!*)

In ***addition*** to the previous examples:

English	*Spanish*	*[Helpful Reminders]*
Abdicative................	Abdicativo	
Abditive....................	Abditivo	
Abirritative...............	Abirritativo	
Abjunctive................	Abjuntivo	
Ablative...................	Ablativo	
Acceptive.................	Aceptivo	[Only 1 C!]
Accretive.................	Acretivo	[Only 1 C!]
Accumulative...........	Acumulativo	[Only 1 C!]
Accusative...............	Acusativo	[Only 1 C!]
Acquisitive...............	Acquisitivo	[also Adquisitivo]
Adjudicative............	Adjudicativo	
Adjunctive................	Adjuntivo	[No C!]
Adjustive.................	Adjustivo	
Administrative..........	Administrativo	
Admissive................	Admisivo	[Only 1 S!]
Admonitive...............	Admonitivo	
Adumbrative.............	Adumbrativo	
Adventive.................	Adventivo	
Adversative..............	Adversativo	
Collusive..................	Colusivo	[Only 1 L!]
Coercive...................	Coercivo	
Cognoscitive.............	Cognositivo	[Quirk # 6!]
Cohortative..............	Cohortativo	[Quirk # 1!]
Commiserative..........	Comiserativo	[Only 1 M!]
Communicative..........	Comunicativo	[Only 1 M!]
Compelative.............	Compelativo	
Compensative...........	Compensativo	
Competitive...............	Competitivo	
Completive...............	Completivo	
Compressive.............	Compresivo	[Only 1 S!]

English	Spanish	[Helpful Reminders]
Compulsa<u>tive</u>............	Compulsa<u>tivo</u>	
Compulsive...............	Compulsivo	
Conative..................	Conativo	
Concentrative...........	Concentrativo	
Conceptive...............	Conceptivo	
Concessive...............	Concesivo	[Only 1 S!]
Conciliative...............	Conciliativo	
Concresive...............	Concresivo	
Conclusive................	Conclusivo	
Concusive................	Concusivo	
Condensative...........	Condensativo	
Conductive...............	Conductivo	
Conducive................	Conducivo	(also Conducente)
Conflagrative...........	Conflagrativo	
Conflictive................	Conflictivo	
Confusive................	Confusivo	
Conglutinative...........	Conglutinativo	
Congretive...............	Cogretivo	
Congressive..............	Congresivo	[Only 1 S!]
Congressive..............	Congresivo	[Only 1 S!]
Conjugative...............	Conjugativo	
Conjunctive...............	Conjuntivo	[No C!]
Connective...............	Conectivo	[Only 1 N!]
Connotative...............	Conotativo	[Only 1 N!]
Consolidative...........	Consolidativo	
Constitutive...............	Constitutivo	
Constrictive...............	Constrictivo	
Constructive.............	Constructivo	
Consultative...............	Consultativo	
Contaminative...........	Contaminativo	
Contemplative...........	Contemplativo	
Continuative.............	Continuativo	
Contractive...............	Contractivo	
Convective...............	Convectivo	
Conversative.............	Conversativo	
Conversive...............	Conversivo	
Convulsive................	Convulsivo	
Cooptative................	Cooptativo	
Coordinative.............	Coordinativo	
Copulative................	Copulativo	
Corporative...............	Corporativo	
Corrective................	Correctivo	
Correlative...............	Correlativo	
Dative......................	Dativo	

Charles Mazal-Cami

English	Spanish	[Helpful Reminders]
Deceptive...............	Deceptivo	
Declarative..............	Declarativo	
Decusative...............	Decusativo	
Decorative...............	Decorativo	
Dedicative...............	Dedicativo	
Deductive...............	Deductivo	
Defunctive...............	Defuntivo	[No C!]
Degenerative...........	Degenerativo	
Degressive...............	Degresivo	[Only 1 S!]
Deletive.................	Deletivo	
Deliberative.............	Deliberativo	
Delineative...............	Delineativo	
Delusive..................	Delusivo	
Demostrative...........	Demostrativo	
Denominative..........	Denominativo	
Denotative...............	Denotativo	
Denunciative...........	Denunciativo	
Deoppulative...........	Deopulativo	[Only 1 P!]
Depletive................	Depletivo	
Deprecative.............	Deprecativo	
Depressive...............	Depresivo	[Only 1 S!]
Depurative...............	Depurativo	
Descensive...............	Descensivo	
Descriptive...............	Descriptivo	
Desiderative.............	Desiderativo	
Designative...............	Designativo	
Desitive..................	Desitivo	
Dessicative..............	Desicativo	[Only 1 S!]
Elective..................	Electivo	
Elusive...................	Elusivo	
Enumerative............	Enumerativo	
Estimative................	Estimativo	
Evasive...................	Evasivo	
Factitive.................	Factitivo	
Factive...................	Factivo	
Federative...............	Federativo	
Fermentative............	Fermentativo	
Fixative..................	Fijativo	[Note J for X!]
Flotative.................	Flotativo	
Fluxive...................	Flujivo	[Note J for X!]
Fotive....................	Fotivo	
Fricative.................	Fricativo	
Fruitive..................	Frutivo	[Note no "UI"!]
Genitive.................	Genitivo	[Quirk # 12]

English	Spanish	*[Helpful Reminders]*
Germina**tive**............	Germina**tivo**	[Quirk # 12]
Gerun**dive**..............	Gerun**divo**	[Quirk # 12]
Hortative................	Hortativo	[Quirk # 1!]
Humective..............	Humectivo	[Quirk # 1!]
Idiorepulsive.........	Idiorepulsivo	
Illative..................	Ilativo	[Only 1 L!]
Illuminative............	Iluminativo	[Only 1 L!]
Imaginative............	Imaginativo	
Imitative...............	Imitativo	
Impassive..............	Impasivo	[Only 1 S!]
Impeditive.............	Impeditivo	
Impressive............	Impresivo	[Only 1 S!]
Impulsive..............	Impulsivo	
Imputative.............	Imputativo	
Inappreciative........	Inapreciativo	[Only 1 P!]
Inapprehensive......	Inaprehensivo	[Only 1 P!]
Incarnative............	Incarnativo	
Inceptive...............	Inceptivo	
Inchoative.............	Incoativo	[No H!]
Incitative..............	Incitativo	
Inclusive...............	Inclusivo	
Incogitative...........	Incogitativo	
Incommunicative.....	Incomunicativo	[Only 1 M!]
Incomprehensive....	Incomprehensivo	
Inconclusive...........	Inconclusivo	
Incrassative...........	Incrasativo	[Only 1 S!]
Incubative.............	Indecisivo	
Indefective............	Indefectivo	
Indescriptive..........	Indescriptivo	
Indicative..............	Indicativo	
Indictive...............	Indictivo	
Indigestive............	Indegistivo	
Indiscrimminative...	Indiscriminativo	[Only 1 M!]
Indistinctive...........	Indistinctivo	
Inductive...............	Inductivo	
Ineffective.............	Inefectivo	[Only 1 F!]
Inexhaustive...........	Inexhaustivo	
Inexplosive.............	Inexplosivo	
Inexpressive...........	Inexpresivo	[Only 1 S!]
Ineffective.............	Inefectivo	[Only 1 F!]
Infective...............	Infectivo	
Infestive...............	Infestivo	
Infiltrative..............	Infiltrativo	
Infinitive...............	Infinitivo	
Infirmative.............	Infirmativo	

Charles Mazal-Cami

English	Spanish	[Helpful Reminders]
Inflammative............	Inflamativo	[Only 1 M!]
Inflective...............	Inflectivo	
Inflexive................	Inflexivo	
Inflictive................	Inflictivo	
Influencive.............	Influencivo	
Influxive................	Influxivo	
Informative............	Informativo	
Infusive..................	Infusivo	
Ingestive...............	Ingestivo	
Inhabitative............	Inhabitativo	[Quirk # 1!]
Inhibitive...............	Inhibitivo	[Quirk # 1!]
Inirritative..............	Inirritativo	
Inobtrusive.............	Inobtrusivo	
Inoculative.............	Inoculativo	
Inoffensive.............	Inofensivo	[Only 1 F!]
Inoperative.............	Inoperativo	
Inopressive.............	Inopresivo	[Only 1 S!]
Inscriptive..............	Inscriptivo	
Insensitive..............	Insensitivo	
Insignificative...........	Insignificativo	
Insinuative..............	Insinuativo	
Inspective..............	Inspectivo	
Instigative.............	Instigativo	
Instinctive..............	Instinctivo	
Institutive..............	Institutivo	
Insusceptive...........	Insusceptivo	
Integrative.............	Integrativo	
Intellective.............	Intelectivo	[Only 1 L!]
Intempestive............	Intempestivo	
Intensative.............	Intensativo	
Intentive................	Intentivo	
Interactive.............	Interactivo	
Interceptive............	Interceptivo	
Interdictive.............	Interdictivo	
Intermissive	Intermisivo	[Only 1 S!]
Internecive.............	Internecivo	
Interoceptive...........	Interoceptivo	
Interpenetrative......	Interpenetrativo	
Interpretive............	Interpretivo	
Interrogative...........	Interrogativo	
Interruptive............	Interruptivo	
Intransitive..............	Intransitivo	
Introductive............	Introductivo	
Introspective...........	Introspectivo	

English	Spanish	[Helpful Reminders]
Introversive.............	Introversivo	
Introvertive.............	Introvertivo	
Intrusive................	Intrusivo	
Intuitive................	Intuitivo	
Intussusceptive........	Intususceptivo	[Only 1 S!]
Invective...............	Invectivo	
Inventive...............	Inventivo	
Inversive...............	Inversivo	
Investigative..........	Investigativo	
Investitive.............	Investitivo	
Invigorative...........	Invigorativo	
Irradiative	Irradiativo	
Irreceptive.............	Irreceptivo	
Irreflective.............	Irreflectivo	
Irrelative...............	Irrelativo	
Irremissive.............	Irremisivo	[Only 1 S!]
Irrespective...........	Irrespectivo	
Irretentive.............	Irretentivo	
Irrigative...............	Irrigativo	
Irritative...............	Irritativo	
Irruptive...............	Irruptivo	
Iterative...............	Iterativo	
Jurisdictive...........	Jurisdictivo	
Jussive................	Jusivo	[Only 1 S!]
Lambative.............	Lambativo	
Laudative.............	Laudativo	
Lenitive................	Lenitivo	
Limitative.............	Limitativo	
Limitive...............	Limitivo	
Liquifactive...........	Liquifactivo	
Locative................	Locativo	
Lustrative.............	Lustrativo	
Manipulative..........	Manipulativo	
Manumotive...........	Manumotivo	
Massive................	Masivo	[Only 1 S!]
Maturative.............	Madurativo	[D for T!]
Mediative.............	Mediativo	
Medicative.............	Medicativo	
Meditative.............	Meditativo	
Meliorative...........	Meliorativo	
Mensurative...........	Mensurativo	
Ministrative...........	Ministrativo	
Mordicative...........	Mordicativo	
Motive.................	Motivo	
Multiplicative.........	Multiplicativo	

English	Spanish	[Helpful Reminders]
Mutative.............	Mutativo	
Mutilative.............	Mutilativo	
Narrative.............	Narrativo	
Nauseative.............	Nauseativo	
Negative.............	Negativo	
Nominative.............	Nominativo	

For English words beginning with the **PREFIX** *"non.."* (as in **non**defensi*ve*),
substitute the **PREFIX** with *"in.."* for the Spanish translation *(in*defensi*vo):*
You can *also* substitute the **English** prefix *"non"* with the Spanish *word "no"*,
making two words: *No defensivo*
(*"no"* of course, means the same in both languages)

English	Spanish	Reminders
Nonassertive.............	Inasertivo	[Only 1 S!]
Nonauthoritative	Inautoritativo	[No H!]
Noncognitive.............	Incognitivo	
Noncohesive.............	Incohesivo	
Noncoercive.............	Incoersivo	
Noncognitive.............	Incognitivo	
Noncollaborative.......	Incolaborativo	[Only 1 L!]
Noncompetitive...........	Incompetitivo	
Nonconnective...........	Inconectivo	[Only 1 N!]
Nonconsecutive	Inconsecutivo	
Nonconservative	Inconservativo	
Nonconstructive	Inconstructivo	
Noncontemplative	Incontemplativo	
Noncooperative	Incooperativo	
Noncorrective...........	Incorrectivo	
Noncorrosive.............	Incorrosivo	
Noncreative.............	Increativo	
Noncummulative	Incomulativo	[Only 1 M!]
Nondeceptive.............	Indeceptivo	
Nondefensive.............	Indefensivo	
Nonderivative...........	Inderivativo	
Nondestructive...........	Indestructivo	
Nondiffractive...........	Indifractivo	[Only 1 F!]
Nondistinctive...........	Indistintivo	[No C!]
Nondistributive.........	Indistributivo	[also Indistribuible]
Noneffective.............	Inefectivo	[Only 1 F!]
Nonelective.............	Inelectivo	
Nonexclusive.............	Inexclusivo	
Nonexecutive.............	Inejecutivo	[J for X! Quirk # 9]
Nonexpansive...........	Inexpansivo	
Nonexplosive.............	Inexplosivo	
Nonfigurative.............	Infigurativo	

English	Spanish	[Helpful Reminders]
Nonfricative.............	Infricativo	
Nongenerative..........	Ingenerativo	
Nonimitative..............	Inimitativo	[also *Inimitable*]
Noninclusive..............	Noinclusivo	[No for In]
Noninductive.............	Noinductivo	[No for In]
Noninformative..........	Noinformativo	[No for In]
Nonobjective.............	Inobjetivo	[No C!]
Nonoperative.............	Inoperativo	
Nonproductive...........	Inproductivo	
Nonprogressive.........	Inprogresivo	[Only 1 S!]
Nonprotective............	Inprotectivo	
Nonreactive...............	Inreactivo	
Nonrelative...............	Inrelativo	
Nonrepresentative ...	Inrepresentativo	
Nonreproductive	Inreproductivo	
Nonrestrictive...........	Inrestrictivo	
Nonretentive............	Inretentivo	
Nonselective............	Inselectivo	
Nonsensitive.............	Insensitivo	[also *Insensible*]
Nonspeculative.........	Inspeculativo	
Nonsubmissive..........	Insubmisivo	[Only 1 S!]
Nonsuccessive..........	Insucesivo	[Only 1 C, S!]
Nonvegetative..........	Invegetativo	
Normative................	Normativo	
Notative...................	Notativo	
Numerative..............	Numerativo	
Nutritive..................	Nutritivo	
Objective.................	Objetivo	[No C!]
Obliterative..............	Obliterativo	
Obstructive...............	Obstructivo	
Obvulative................	Obvulativo	
Occasive..................	Ocasivo	[Only 1 C!]
Occupative..............	Ocupativo	[Only 1 C!]
Olive......[the tree]....	Olivo	
Olive......[the color]...	Oliva	
Olive......[the fruit].....	Oliva	[also Aceituna]
Ommisive..................	Omisivo	[Only 1 M!]
Omnispective.............	Omnipesctive	
Opiniative.................	Opiniativo	
Oppositive................	Opositivo	[Only 1 P!]
Oppressive................	Opresivo	[Only 1 P, S!]
Ordinative.................	Ordinativo	
Originative................	Origenativo	
Oscilative.................	Oscilativo	
Ostensive.................	Ostensivo	
Ostentive..................	Ostentivo	

Charles Mazal-Cami

English	Spanish	[Helpful Reminders]
Oxidative...................	Oxidativo	
Palliative...................	Paliativo	[Only 1 L!]
Partitive.....................	Partitivo	
Parturitive.................	Parturitivo	
Passive......................	Pasivo	[Only 1 S!]
Pedonotive................	Pedonotivo	
Pejorative..................	Pejorativo	
Pendentive.................	Pendentivo	
Penetrative................	Penetrativo	
Percussive..................	Percusivo	[Only 1 S!]
Perfective.................	Perfectivo	
Perforative................	Perforativo	
Perfusive..................	Perfusivo	
Permissive.................	Permisivo	[Only one S!]
Persecutive..............	Persecutivo	
Persistive.................	Persistivo	
Perspective..............	Perspectiva	[Fem. Gender]
Perspirative..............	Perspirativo	
Persuasive.................	Persuasivo	
Perturbative..............	Perturbativo	
Philoprogenitive	Filoprogenitivo	[F for PH! Quirk # 5!]
Photosensitive...........	Fotosensitivo	[also Fotosensible]
Pignorative................	Pignorativo	
Placative...................	Aplacativo	[A before P!]
Portentive.................	Portentivo	
Possessive................	Posesivo	[No dbl. S!]

For English words with the **PREFIX** *"post.."*,
substitute with *"pos.."* for the Spanish translation.

Postoperative..............	Posoperativo	
Postpositive................	Pospositivo	
Potestative.................	Potestativo	
Precative	Precativo	
Preceptive..................	Preceptivo	
Preclusive..................	Preclusivo	
Precursive..................	Precursivo	
Predecessive..............	Predecesivo	[Only 1 S!]
Predestinative.............	Predestinativo	
Predicative.................	Predicativo	
Predictive..................	Predictivo	
Preemptive................	Preemptivo	
Preformative..............	Preformativo	
Prejudicative..............	Prejudicativo	
Prelusive...................	Prelusivo	
Premeditative.............	Premeditativo	

English	Spanish	[Helpful Reminders]
Prepartive...............	Prepartivo	
Preparative..............	Preparativo	
Prepositive..............	Prepositivo	
Prerogative.............	Prerogativo	
Prescriptive	Prescriptivo	
Presentative..............	Presentativo	
Presentive...............	Presentivo	
Preservative.............	Preservativo	
Presumptive.............	Presuntivo	[Note diff. Sp.]
Pretentative..............	Pretentativo	
Preventative.............	Preventativo	
Preventive...............	Preventivo	
Primitive.................	Primitivo	
Privative	Privativo	
Probative................	Probativo	
Procreative..............	Procreativo	
Productive...............	Productivo	
Profusive................	Profusivo	[also Profuso]
Progressive..............	Progresivo	[Only 1 S!]
Prohibitive..............	Prohibitivo	
Pronunciative...........	Pronunciativo	
Propagative.............	Propagativo	
Propitiative..............	Propiciativo	[C for T!]
Proprioceptive...........	Proprioceptivo	
Propulsive...............	Propulsivo	
Proscriptive.............	Proscriptivo	
Prospective.............	Prospectivo	
Protective...............	Protectivo	
Protractive	Protractivo	
Protrusive...............	Protrusivo	
Provocative..............	Provocativo	
Punitive.................	Punitivo	
Punctuative.............	Puntuativo	[Note no C!]
Purgative................	Purgativo	
Purificative.............	Purificativo	
Putative.................	Putativo	
Putrefactive.............	Putrefactivo	
Qualificative.............	Calificativo	[Note diff. sp.!]
Qualitative..............	Cualitativo	[C for Q!]
Quantitative.............	Cuantitativo	[C for Q!]
Quidative................	Quidativo	
Quidditative.............	Quiditativo	[Only 1 D!]
Radiative................	Radiativo	
Radioactive.............	Radioactivo	
Radiosensitive...........	Radiosensitivo	[also Radiosensible]

English	*Spanish*	*[Helpful Reminders]*
Ratiocinative	Raciocinativo	[C for T!]
Reactive	Reactivo	
Recapitulative	Recapitulativo	
Receptive	Receptivo	
Recessive	Recesivo	[Only 1 S!]
Reciprocative	Reciprocativo	
Recitative	Recitativo	
Reclusive	Reclusivo	
Recollective	Recolectivo	[Only 1 L!]
Recommendative	Recomendativo	[Only 1 M!]
Recompensive	Recompensivo	
Reconstructive	Reconstructivo	
Recreative	Recreativo	
Recuperative	Recuperativo	
Recusative	Recusativo	
Redditive	Reditivo	[Only 1 D!]
Redemptive	Redemptivo	
Reductive	Reductivo	
Refective	Refectivo	
Reflective	Reflectivo	
Reflexive	Reflexivo	
Reformative	Reformativo	
Refractive	Refractivo	
Regenerative	Regenerativo	
Regressive	Regresivo	[Only 1 S!]
Regulative	Regulativo	
Reiterative	Reiterativo	
Relative.... (adjective)	Relativo	
Remissive	Remisivo	[Only 1 S!]
Remunerative	Remunerativo	
Reparative	Reparativo	
Repercussive	Repercusivo	[Only 1 S!]
Repetitive	Repetitivo	
Repletive	Repletivo	
Replicative	Replicativo	
Reprehensive	Reprehensivo	[Quirk # 1!]
Representative	Representativo	
Repressive	Represivo	[Only 1 S!]
Reproductive	Reproductivo	
Repulsive	Repulsivo	
Requisitive	Requisitivo	
Rescriptive	Rescriptivo	
Resentive	Resentivo	
Reservative	Reservativo	

English	Spanish	[Helpful Reminders]
Resist*ive*	Resist*ivo*	
Resolutive	Resolutivo	
Resorptive	Resorbtivo	[B for P!]
Respective	Respectivo	
Respirative	Respirativo	
Responsive	Responsivo	
Restitutive	Restitutivo	
Restrictive	Restrictivo	
Resultive	Resultivo	
Resumptive	Resumptivo	
Resuscitative	Resucitativo	[Only 1 S!]
Retaliative	Retaliativo	
Retardative	Retardativo	
Retentive	Retentivo	
Retortive	Retortivo	
Retractive	Retractivo	
Retributive	Retributivo	
Retroactive	Retroactivo	
Retrogenerative	Retrogenerativo	
Retrogressive	Retrogresivo	[Only 1 S!]
Retrooperative	Retrooperativo	
Retropulsive	Retropulsivo	
Retrospective	Retrospectivo	
Reverberative	Reverberativo	
Revertive	Revertivo	
Revolutive	Revolutivo	
Revulsive	Revulsivo	
Rotative	Rotativo	
Ruminative	Ruminativo	
Ruptive	Ruptivo	
Sanative	Sanativo	
Seclusive	Seclusivo	
Sedative	Sedativo	
Sensitive	Sensitivo	[Also *Sensible*]
Separative	Separativo	
Simulative	Simulativo	
Speculative	Especulativo	[Quirk # 6!]
Stimulative	Estimulativo	[Quirk # 6!]
Stipulative	Estipulativo	[Quirk # 6!]
Stupecative	Estupefactivo	[also *Estupefaciente*]
Suasive	Esuasivo	[Quirk # 6!]
Subdivisive	Subdivisivo	
Subjective	Sujetivo	[No B or C!]
Submissive	Submisivo	[Only 1 S!]
Subordinative	Subordinativo	
Subscriptive	Subscriptivo	

Charles Mazal-Cami

English	Spanish	[Helpful Reminders]
Substantiat*ive*..........	Sustanciat**ivo**	[S for B!]
Substantive...............	Sustantivo	[S for B!]
Substitutive..............	Sustitutivo	[S for B!]
Subsumptive..............	Subsumptivo	
Successive................	Sucesivo	[1 C, 1 S!]
Suffusive.................	Sufusivo	[Only 1 F!]
Superconductive	Superconductivo	
Supersensitive..........	Supersensitivo	[Also *Supersensible*]
Superssesive............	Supersesivo	[Only 1 S!]
Suppletive................	Supletivo	[Only 1 P!]
Supplicative	Suplicativo	[Only 1 P!]
Supportive...............	Soportivo	[O for U, 1 P!]
Subpositive..............	Subpositivo	
Suppressive..............	Supresivo	[1 P, 1 S!]
Suppurative...............	Supurativo	[Only 1 P!]
Susceptive................	Susceptivo	
Suspensive...............	Suspensivo	
Sustentative	Sustentativo	
Temulentive..............	Temulentivo	
Terminative..............	Terminativo	
Titilative...................	Titilativo	
Tolerative.................	Tolerativo	
Tortive......................	Tortivo	
Totitive.....................	Totitivo	
Tractive....................	Tractivo	
Traditive...................	Traditivo	
Transcriptive.............	Transcriptivo	
Transformative..........	Transformativo	
Transfugitive.............	Transfugitivo	
Transfusive...............	Transfusivo	
Transgressive............	Transgresivo	[Only 1 S!]
Transitive.................	Transitivo	
Transmissive.............	Transmisivo	[Only 1 S!]
Transmutative...........	Transmutativo	
Transpositive............	Transpositivo	
Tussive.....................	Tusivo	[Only 1 S!]
Ulcerative................	Ulcerativo	
Ultraconservative	Ultraconservativo	[also Ultraconservador]

For English words beginning with the **PREFIX** *"un.."* (as in *un*agress*ive*), *substitute* with *"in.."* for the Spanish translation, *in*agres*ivo*.

Unaggress*ive*..............	Inagres**ivo**	
Unappreciative...........	Inapreciativo	[Only 1 P!]
Unargumentative	Inargumentativo	

English	Spanish	[Helpful Reminders]
Unattrac**tive**...............	Inatract**ivo**	
Unauthoritative............	Inautoritativo	[No "TH"!]
Unconservative...........	Inconservativo	[also *Inconservador*]
Uncooperative............	Incooperativo	
Unimaginative.............	Inimaginativo	
Uninquisitive..............	Noinquisitivo	["No" for "In"!]
Uninventive................	Noinventivo	["No" for "In"!]
Unobtrusive...............	Inobtrusivo	
Unoffensive...............	Inofensivo	[Only 1 F!]
Unparticipative	Inparticipativo	
Unpersuasive.............	Inpersuasivo	
Unpositive................	Inpositivo	
Unprogressive...........	Inprogresivo	[Only 1 S!]
Unreceptive..............	Inreceptivo	
Unremunerative.........	Inremunerativo	
Unrepresentative	Inrepresentativo	
Unresponsive.............	Inresponsivo	
Unseductive...............	Inseductivo	
Unselective...............	Inselectivo	
Unspeculative...........	Inespeculativo	[Quirk # 6!]
Unsubmissive.............	Insubmisivo	[Only 1 S!]
Unsuccesssive...........	Insucesivo	[1 C, 1 S!]
Unsuggestive.............	Insugestivo	[Only 1 G!]
Unapprehensive........	Inaprehensivo	[Only 1 P!]
Uncommunicative.......	Incomunicativo	[Only 1 M!]
Undecisive................	Indecisivo	
Undemonstrative	Indemostrativo	[No N!]
Undulative................	Indulativo	
Unexpressive.............	Inexpresivo	[Only 1 S!]
Unproductive............	Inproductivo	
Urinative..................	Orinativo	[O for U!]
Usitative...................	Usitativo	
Vasifactive................	Vasifactivo	
Vegetative................	Vegetativo	
Vellicative................	Velicativo	[Only 1 L!]
Venerative................	Venerativo	[also *Venerable* see BLE Rule]
Vengative.................	Vengativo	
Ventilative................	Ventilativo	
Verificative...............	Verificativo	
Vetitive.....................	Vetitivo	
Vibrative...................	Vibrativo	
Vindicative................	Vindicativo	
Vindictive.................	Vindictivo	
Violative...................	Violativo	
Visive.......................	Visivo	

Charles Mazal-Cami

English	Spanish	[Helpful Reminders]
Vituperat*ive*..............	Vituperat**ivo**	
Vivic**ative**..................	Vivicat**ivo**	
Voc**ative**..................	Vocat**ivo**	
Vol**itive**....................	Volit**ivo**	
Vom**itive**..................	Vomit**ivo**	
Vot**ive**........................	Vot**ivo**	

Notable Exceptions:

Attent*ive*..................	Atento	
Conduc**ive**.................	Conducente	
Conservat**ive**.............	Conservador	
Insensit**ive**.................	Insensible	
Perversi**ve**.................	Perverso	
Petrifact*ive*...............	Petrifacto	
Photosens**itive**..........	Fotosensible	
Profus**ive**...................	Profuso	
Relat*ive*...... (parental)	Pariente	[cousins, uncles, etc.]
Supersens**itive**..........	Supersensible	
Ultraconservat**ive**.....	Ultraconservador	
Unattent**ive**...............	Inatento	

We can forego the Practice Session!

You were not expected to have actually read *each and every word example* set forth in the preceding chapters! If you have a fairly good command of the English language, you already *knew* most of the words and you had only to learn the *Rules* that applied to the word *endings*.

These word examples are intended only to give you a visual recognition of *English* words with each of the word endings. If you have learned all of the preceding Rules *and* have read each of the word examples with the Spanish translations and *still* have reached this point in the book in twenty minutes, then you deserve recognition and considerable admiration for your skill. *You also ought to be on TV!*

In the following Chapter, you will find far fewer word examples for each of the **twenty-six *Minor Rules*.** You can add a few thousand *more* words to your Spanish vocabulary by learning the Minor Rules. Now that you are no longer racing with the clock to come in under twenty - minutes, you should be able to continue at a more leisurely pace!

> "For learning, the eye is more useful than the ear and the mouth is of no use whatsoever."
>
> Ancient Proverb

We wouldn't want to take issue with Mr. A. Proverb over that statement, certainly not when it comes to the eye, the specific organ for which this book was designed. However, denigrating the mouth is going just a bit too far, particularly since we have made a real commotion here about pronunciation! It is obvious that Mr. Proverb did not have a copy of this book at hand when he issued that pronouncement. We will stick with our guns and suggest once again that you practice pronouncing the Spanish vowels, out loud and often. Your *ear* will let you know how you are progressing. For those of you who do not have the opportunity of practicing with a Spanish-speaking audience, an audiotape version of this book will be available soon.

Palabra Press welcomes your comments and invites you to drop us a note. Even if you did not know a *single word* in Spanish before you opened this book, you should review what you have learned thusfar and perhaps convince yourself that you can (and do) recognize and understand more Spanish words now than many who have taken formal courses in the language for years!

There are more words to be learned in the following Chapter and still more in the Appendix and, although knowing as many words in Spanish as you now do puts you away out in front, you must still learn how to *use* them. Beginning with Chapter Eighteen, you will learn about word *genders* (at last!), how to conjugate verbs (all of those, for example, that you learned in Chapters Three and Four) and forming simple sentences in past, present and future tenses. So, just because you have learned twenty thousand words or so in Spanish, DON'T STOP NOW!

CHAPTER SIXTEEN

The **MINOR** Rules

(26 of them!)

Now that we have covered the Major Rules and you have learned *many thousands* of words in Spanish, we will celebrate the occasion by looking at the **Minor Rules** (and learning a few more thousand words). These Rules are "Minor" because either:

(a)　There are fewer words in English to which they apply than the Major Rules, *or*

(b)　There are more exceptions than there are in the Major Rules, *or*

(c)　Both of the above.

The object here is to further illustrate the intriguing similarity between English and Spanish. You can memorize these **Minor Rules** if you are so inclined. After all, each time you memorize a Rule, you increase your vocabulary by a *phenomenal multiple* (Spanish: múltiple fenomenal) and that is what this book is about! However, if you aren't quite that zealous, you can simply refer to the *Cheat Sheet* at the end of the Appendix.

For the sake of convenience and easy reference, the Minor Rules appear in alphabetical order, and not in the order of their importance.

Keep in mind that these Rules, in the great majority of the cases, apply to words in English having two or more syllables!

So, *hold on*...here we go!

English	Spanish	HelpfulReminders

 # 1

....AR	....AR	
Angul**ar**............	Angul**ar**	
Annular............	Anular	[Only 1 N!]
Articular...........	Articular	
Auricular..........	Auricular	
Binocular..........	Binocular	
Circular............	Circular	
Collar...............	Collar	Quirk # 3!]
Insular..............	Insular	
Linear..............	Linear	
Modular...........	Modular	
Molar...............	Molar	
Muscular..........	Muscular	
Ocular..............	Ocular	
Perpendicular...	Perpendicular	
Pillar................	Pilar	[Only 1 L!]
Polar................	Polar	
Popular............	Popular	
Sonar...............	Sonar	
Triangular.........	Triangular	
Vascular...........	Vascular	

 # 2

....ATOR	....ADOR	
Acceler**ator**.......	Aceler**ador**	[No double C!]
Accumul**ator**......	Acumul**ador**	[No double C!]
Attenu**ator**.........	Atenu**ador**	[Only 1 T!]
Avi**ator**..............	Avi**ador**	
Calibr**ator**..........	Calibr**ador**	
Corrug**ator**.........	Corrug**ador**	
Cre**ator**..............	Cre**ador**	

....ATOR	....ADOR	
Dict**ator**............	Dict**ador**	
Elev**ator**...........	Eleva**dor**	
Equ**ator**............	Ecu**ador**	[C for Q!]
Fabric**ator**..........	Fabric**ador**	
Gladi**ator**...........	Gladi**ador**	
Initi**ator**............	Ini**ciador**	[C for T!]
Instig**ator**...........	Instig**ador**	
Lubric**ator**..........	Lubric**ador**	
Medi**ator**............	Medi**ador**	
Narr**ator**............	Narr**ador**	
Navig**ator**...........	Nave**gador**	[E for I!]
Oper**ator**...........	Oper**ador**	
Or**ator**...............	Or**ador**	
Origin**ator**..........	Origin**ador**	
Oxygen**ator**........	Oxigen**ador**	[i for y!]
Radi**ator**............	Radi**ador**	
Refriger**ator**.......	Refriger**ador**	
Sen**ator**.............	Sen**ador**	
Simul**ator**...........	Simul**ador**	

3

....CLE	....CULO	
Arti**cle**.............	Artí**culo**	
Mono**cle**...........	Monó**culo**	
Ora**cle**.............	Orá**culo**	
Specta**cle**..........	Espectá**culo**	[Quirk # 6!]
Tenta**cle**...........	Tentá**culo**	
Testi**cle**............	Testí**culo**	

Exception:

Mira**cle**............	Milagro

4

....COPY   ....COPIA

English	Spanish	
Arthros**copy**.......	Artros**copía**	[Quirk # 1!]
Copy................	**Cópia**	
Endos**copy**.........	Endos**copía**	
Fluoros**copy**.......	Fluoros**copía**	
Micros**copy**........	Micros**copía**	
Spectros**copy**......	Espectros**copía**	[Quirk # 6!]

5

....CTOR   ....CTOR

English	Spanish	
A**ctor**................	A**ctor**	
Colle**ctor**...........	Cole**ctor**	[Only 1 L!]
Condu**ctor**..........	Condu**ctor**	
Conne**ctor**..........	Cone**ctor**	[Only 1 N!]
Contra**ctor**.........	Contra**ctor**	(also Contratista)
Corre**ctor**...........	Corre**ctor**	
Dete**ctor**...........	Decte**ctor**	
Dire**ctor**............	Dire**ctor**	
Do**ctor**.............	Do**ctor**	
Fa**ctor**..............	Fa**ctor**	
Inje**ctor**.............	Inye**ctor**	[Y for J!]
Inspe**ctor**...........	Inspe**ctor**	
Instru**ctor**..........	Instru**ctor**	
Prote**ctor**...........	Prote**ctor**	
Rea**ctor**.............	Rea**ctor**	
Re**ctor**..............	Re**ctor**	
Refle**ctor**...........	Refle**ctor**	
Refra**ctor**...........	Refra**ctor**	
Retra**ctor**...........	Retra**ctor**	
Se**ctor**..............	Se**ctor**	
Sele**ctor**............	Sele**ctor**	
Tra**ctor**.............	Tra**ctor**	
Ve**ctor**..............	Ve**ctor**	

6

....ENCE   ....ENCIA

English	Spanish	
Depend**ence**......	Depend**encia**	
Ess**ence**............	Es**encia**	[Only 1 S!]
Evid**ence**..........	Evid**encia**	
Fluoresc**ence**.....	Fluores**encia**	[No SC!]
Independ**ence**....	Independ**encia**	
Jurisprud**ence**.....	Jurisprud**encia**	
Luminesc**ence**....	Lumines**encia**	[No SC!]
Prefer**ence**.........	Prefer**encia**	
Prud**ence**..........	Prud**encia**	
Refer**ence**..........	Refer**encia**	
Sequ**ence**..........	Secu**encia**	[C for Q!]

7

....ENE   ....ENO

English	Spanish	
Acetyl**ene**..........	Acetil**eno**	[I for Y!]
Ethyl**ene**............	Etil**eno**	[No H!]
Methyl**ene**.........	Metil**eno**	[I for Y!]
Poliethyl**ene**......	Polietil**eno**	[I for Y!]
Ser**ene**..............	Ser**eno**	
Tolu**ene**............	Tolu**eno**	

8

....GRAPH   ....GRAFO

English	Spanish	
Electrocardio**graph**....	Electrocardió**grafo**	
Electroencephalo**graph**	Electroencefaló**grafo**	
Encephalo**graph**........	Encefaló**grafo**	[F for PH!]
Metalo**graph**.............	Metaló**grafo**	
Phono**graph**..............	Fonó**grafo**	[F for PH!]
Poly**graph**.................	Polí**grafo**	[I for Y, F for PH!]
Serio**graph**...............	Serió**grafo**	

9

....GRAPHY   ....GRAFIA

English	Spanish	Helpful Reminders
Angio**graphy**......	Angio**grafía**	
Calli**graphy**........	Cali**grafía**	[Only 1 L!]
Geo**graphy**.........	Geo**grafía**	
Micro**graphy**......	Micro**grafía**	[F for PH!]
Ortho**graphy**......	Orto**grafía**	[no "th" in Spanish!]
Photo**graphy**......	Foto**grafía**	[F for PH!]
Topo**graphy**.......	Topo**grafía**	
Xero**graphy**.......	Xero**grafía**	

10

....ICAL   ....ICO

English	Spanish	
Bacteriolog**ical**....	Bacteriológ**ico**	
Econom**ical**..........	Económ**ico**	
Eth**ical**................	Ét**ico**	[No H!]
Log**ical**...............	Lóg**ico**	
Mag**ical**..............	Mág**ico**	
Med**ical**..............	Méd**ico**	
Method**ical**..........	Metód**ico**	[Quirk # 1!]
Exception:		
Rad**ical**...............	**Radical**	[See AL Rule]

11

....IFY   ....IFICAR

[These are all verbs, i.e. *to* Amplify - see Chapt. 18]

English	Spanish	
Ampl**ify**.................	Ampl**ificar**	
Clar**ify**..................	Clar**ificar**	
Class**ify**.................	Clas**ificar**	[only 1 S!]
Ed**ify**......................	Ed**ificar**	
Grat**ify**..................	Grat**ificar**	

#11 (cont)

....IFY	....IFICAR	
Justify	Justificar	
Mollify	Molificar	[Only 1 L!]
Nullify	Nulificar	[Only 1 L!]
Nutrify	Nutrificar	
Pacify	Pacificar	
Ratify	Ratificar	
Solidify	Solidificar	
Tipify	Tipificar	
Unify	Unificar	
Verify	Verificar	

12

....INE	....INA	
(and add an "R" for verbs)		
Decline	Declinar	[verb]
Gasoline	Gasolina	
Recline	Reclinar	[verb]
Refine	Refinar	[verb]
Tetracycline	Tetraciclina	[I for Y!]

13

....IST	....ISTA	
Antagonist	Antagonista	
Assist	Asista	[Only 1 S!]
Chorist	Corista	[no H!]
Columnist	Columnista	
Communist	Comunista	[Only 1 M!]
Congregationalist	Congregacionalista	[c for t!]
Dentist	Dentista	
Desist	Desista	
Florist	Florista	
List	Lista	
Medalist	Medalista	
Nationalist	Nacionalista	[c for t!]

....IST   ....ISTA

Occulist............	Oculista	[Only 1 C!]
Organist............	Organista	
Populist............	Populista	
Pugilist............	Pugilista	
Rentist............	Rentista	
Resist............	Resista	
Socialist............	Socialista	
Specialist...........	Especialista	[Quirk # 6]
Subsist............	Subsista	

Exceptions:

Twist............	Torcer	[verb]
List *[to lean]*....	Reclinar	[verb]
Consist............	Consistir	
Mist............	Neblina	
Druggist...........	Farmacólogo	

14

....IUM   ....IO

Actinium............	Actinio	
Aluminium (Brit. Sp.)...	Aluminio	
Gallium............	Galio	[Only 1 L!]
Medium............	Medio	
Palladium............	Paladio	[Only 1 L!]
Podium............	Podio	
Premium............	Premio	
Rhodium............	Rodio	[no "RH" in Spanish!]
Selenium............	Selenio	
Sodium............	Sodio	
Stadium............	Estadio	[Quirk # 6!]
Xirconium............	Xirconio	

Exceptions:

Chromium............	Cromo	
Cranium............		Craneo

15

....LOGY   ....LOGIA

English	Spanish	Helpful Reminders
Ana**logy**	Ana**logía**	
Anthropo**logy**	Antropo**logía**	[Quirk # 1!]
Astro**logy**	Astro**logía**	
Bio**logy**	Bio**logía**	
Cancero**logy**	Cancero**logía**	
Eco**logy**	Eco**logía**	
Entomo**logy**	Entomo**logía**	
Geo**logy**	Geo**logía**	
Methodo**logy**	Metodo**logía**	[Quirk # 1!]
Morpho**logy**	Morfo**logía**	[no PH!]
Ophthalmo**logy**	Oftalmo**logía**	[Quirk # 1, 5!]
Paleonto**logy**	Paleonto**logía**	
Physio**logy**	Fisio**logía**	[no PH, i for y!]
Tri**logy**	Tri**logía**	
Viro**logy**	Viro**logía**	
Vulcano**logy**	Vulcano**logía**	
Zoo**logy**	Zoo**logía**	[Diphthong!]

Exceptions:

English	Spanish
Apo**logy**	Disculpa
Eu**logy**	Elogio

16

....METER   ....METRO

English	Spanish	Helpful Reminders
Baro**meter**	Baró**metro**	
Calori**meter**	Calorí**metro**	
Kilo**meter**	Kiló**metro**	
Meter	**Metro**	
Odo**meter**	Odó**metro**	
Photo**meter**	Fotó**metro**	[F for PH!]
Spectrophoto**meter**	Espectrofotó**metro**	[Quirk # 6!]
Sphygmomano**meter**	Esfigmomanó**metro**	[Quirk # 6!]
Thermo**meter**	Termó**metro**	[No H!]

17

....METRY	....METRIA

English	Spanish	Helpful Reminders
Bio**metry**............	Bio**metría**	
Geo**metry**...........	Geo**metría**	
Optho**metry**......	Opto**metría**	[Quirk # 1, 5!]
Ortho**metry**.........	Orto**metría**	[Quirk # 1!]
Poli**metry**............	Poli**metría**	

18

....OMY	....OMIA

English	Spanish	Helpful Reminders
Agron**omy**...........	Agron**omía**	
Anat**omy**.............	Anat**omía**	
Appendect**omy**....	Apendect**omía**	[Only 1 P!]
Auton**omy**...........	Auton**omía**	
Colost**omy**..........	Colost**omía**	
Hysterect**omy**......	Histerect**omía**	[I for Y!]
Mastect**omy**........	Mastect**omía**	
Physion**omy**........	Fision**omía**	[Quirk # 5!]

19

....OR *other* than ....ATOR	....OR
and ....CTOR	

[Remember: 2 or more syllables only!]

English	Spanish	Helpful Reminders
Anteri**or**...........	Anteri**or**	
Cand**or**.............	Cand**or**	
Col**or**..............	Col**or**	
Edit**or**.............	Edit**or**	
Exteri**or**..........	Exteri**or**	
Fav**or**..............	Fav**or**	
Fur**or**..............	Fur**or**	
Hon**or**.............	Hon**or**	[Quirk # 1!]
Horr**or**.............	Horr**or**	[Quirk # 1!]

....OR *other* than ....<u>A</u>TOR   ....OR
and ....<u>C</u>TOR

[Remember: 2 or more syllables only!]

Humor..............	Humor	[Quirk # 1!]
Inferior............	Inferior	
Inventor............	Inventor	
Labor [noun].......	Labor	
Monitor............	Monitor	
Motor...............	Motor	
Pastor...............	Pastor	
Rotor................	Rotor	
Sensor..............	Sensor	
Servomotor........	Servomotor	
Stupor..............	Estupor	[E before ST!]
Successor..........	Sucesor	[Only 1 C, 1 S!]
Superior............	Superior	
Terror...............	Terror	
Transistor	Transistor	
Tumor..............	Tumor	
Valor................	Valor	
Vapor	Vapor [also means Steam]	
Vigor................	Vigor	
Visor.................	Visor	

Exceptions:

Sculptor.............	Escultor
Grantor.............	Subventor

20

....OSIS   ....OSIS

Halit**osis**............	Halit**ósis**	[Quirk # 1!]
Metamorph**osis**...	Metamorf**ósis**	[F for PH!]
Mit**osis**..............	Mit**ósis**	
Neur**osis**............	Neur**ósis**	
Osteopor**osis**.......	Osteopor**ósis**	
Thromb**osis**........	Tromb**ósis**	[No H!]

21

....PLASM   ....PLASMA

Bio**plasm**............	Bio**plásma**
Cata**plasm**..........	Cata**plásma**
Ecto**plasm**..........	Ecto**plásma**
Proto**plasm**.........	Proto**plásma**

For ....SM endings <u>other</u> *than ....PLASM,*
add an "O" for Spanish Translation:
(Also, see Chapter Eight, the ISM Rule)

Orga<u>sm</u>..............	Orga<u>smo</u>	
Spa<u>sm</u>................	Espa<u>smo</u>	[Quirk # 6!]

22

....SCOPE   ....SCOPIO

Cardio**scope**......	Cardio**scópio**	
Endo**scope**.........	Endo**scópio**	
Gastro**scope**.......	Gastro**scópio**	
Micro**scope**........	Micro**scópio**	
Ophthalmo**scope**.	Oftalmo**scópio**	[F for PH, no TH!]
Oto**scope**...........	Oto**scópio**	
Tele**scope**..........	Tele**scópio**	

23

....STY   ....STIA

Dyna<u>sty</u>.............	Dina**stía**
Mode**sty**.............	Mode**stía**
Trave**sty**.............	Trave**stía**

#24

....UME   ....UMIR

Assume............	Asumir	[Only 1 S!]
Consume...........	Consumir	
Exume..............	Exumir	
Presume...........	Presumir	
Resume............	Resumir	

25

....URE   ....URA

Adventure.........	Aventura	[Note no D!]
Aperture...........	Apertura	
Architecture.......	Arquitectura	[Qui for Ch!]
Denture.............	Dentura	
Censure............	Censura	
Conjecture.........	Conjetura	[No "C"!]
Cure.................	Cura	
Fracture............	Fractura	
Future..............	Futura	(or Futuro)
Lecture.............	Lectura	
Manufacture.......	Manufactura	
Mature..............	Madura	[Note D for T!]
Nomenclature.....	Nomenclatura	
Nurture.............	Nurtura	
Overture...........	Overtura	
Pasture.............	Pastura	
Pure.................	Pura	
Rupture.............	Ruptura	
Stature..............	Estatura	[Quirk # 6!]
Suture...............	Sutura	
Tenure.............	Tenura	
Torture.............	Tortura	
Venture.............	Ventura	

25 (cont.)

....URE	....URA

Exceptions:

English	Spanish	
Lure (for fishing)...	Curricán	
Lure (verb)..........	Atraer	(means *"To attract"*)
Manure..............	Estiercol	
Secure..[verb]........	Asegurar	
Sure...................	Seguro	
Vulture*..............	Pájaro de rapiña (wow!)	

| ***A Buzzard is a ...** | **Zopilóte !** | [see Page *viii*] |

26

....UTE	....UTO

English	Spanish	
Ast<u>ute</u>..............	Ast<u>uto</u>	
Convol**ute**.........	Convol**uto**	
Dil**ute**....[adj.]......	Dil**uto**	[also, "Diluido"]
Min**ute**..............	Min**uto**	
Prostit**ute**..........	Prostit**uto**	[male]
	Prostit**uta**	[female]
Resol**ute**............	Resol**uto**	
Stat**ute**..............	Estat**uto**	[Quirk # 6!]

Exceptions:

English	Spanish
Dilute...[verb]........	Diluir
Salute...[verb]........	Saludar
Pollute...[verb].....	Poluir
Refute...[verb]........	Refutar

And there are still *others*, but by now you have probably reached the point of *tot**al** satura**tion**!* (*Sp.* satura**ción** tot**al**)

MISSION ACCOMPLISHED!

The following part of this book is intended to teach you what you can *do* with what you have already learned. Knowing *thousands* of words in Spanish has given you a head-start on learning the language, but it is only logical that you should want to be able to express yourself in more than one-word sentences!

CHAPTER SEVENTEEN

GENDERS & ARTICLES

At last! You have probably been waiting for this with baited breath!
Yes, in Spanish, as in most other languages, there are *masculine* and
feminine-gendered words.

This applies only to **nouns** and their adjectives (modifiers). *Don't panic!*
It isn't really that complicated.   Here are the basic rules:

Masculine-gendered *nouns* are **preceded** by the Article **"el"**
(equivalent to "the" in English)

Thus, **the** piano, in Spanish is **"el** piano".

Feminine-gendered *nouns* are preceded by the Article **"la"**
(*also* equivalent to "the" in English).

the bed , in Spanish is **"la** cama".

Here's how to recognize the gender :

[1] Singular *nouns* in Spanish that *end* in   ..**a**, ..**er** or ..**ción**,
are *feminine* [f].

la puert**a**	[*the* door]
la muj**er**	[*the* woman]
la na**ción**	[*the* nation]

For euphony, use **el** and *not* **la** for feminine *singular* nouns that *begin* with "a..", or "ha..". This avoids using two "a" sounds next to eachother. The equivalent English rule would be
"an apple" instead of *"a apple"*.

Here are some Spanish examples:

el <u>ag</u>ua	[*the* water]
el <u>ha</u>cha	[*the* hatchet]
el <u>a</u>lma	[*the* soul]

These are all *femenine* nouns inasmuch as they *end* in "..a". Using the article "el" does not change the *gender* of these nouns, and the *plural* reverts to the feminine article again, thus:

las aguas	[*the* waters]
las hachas	[*the* hatchets]
las almas	[*the* souls]

[2] Singular nouns in Spanish with endings *other* than the above, are *masculine* [m]. These include nouns that *end* in
"..e", "..en", "..il", "..o", "..or", and "..on"
(*except* ...**CI**ON).

el hombr<u>e</u>	[*the* man]
el tr<u>en</u>	[*the* train]
el mast<u>il</u>	[*the* mast]
el pian<u>o</u>	[*the* piano]
el señ<u>or</u>	[*the* Mister]
el cord<u>ón</u>	[*the* chord]

Nouns designating days, months, and languages are also **masculine***:*

el dia	[*the* day]
el lunes	[*the* monday]
el mes	[*the* month]
el Español	[*the* Spanish]
el Inglés	[*the* English]

Charles Mazal-Cami

[3] The *plural femenine* article is **"las"**

las naciones   [*the* nations]

[4] The *plural masculine* article is **"los"**

los pianos   [*the* pianos]

These, together with the **neuter article** "**lo**" comprise the *Definitive Articles* in Spanish. "**lo**" is used in conjunction with an adjective. In *English*, of course, it is always "*the* (best, highest, longest, etc.)"
For example:

lo mejor del artículo....(*the best part of* the article...)
lo mas alto del edificio....(*the highest part of* the building...)

[5] *This, That, These & Those* are expressed in Spanish
as **este** (or **esta**), **ese** (or **esa**), **estos** (or **estas**)
and **aquellos** (or **aquellas**).

este momento	[*this* moment]	[m]
esta manzana	[*this* apple]	[f]
ese momento	[*that* moment]	[m]
esa manzana	[*that* apple]	[f]
estos momentos	[*these* moments]	[m]
estas manzanas	[*these* apples]	[f]
esos momentos	[*those* moments]	[m]
esas manzanas	[*those* apples]	[f]

Aquellos (or **Aquellas**) is generally used when referring to people
(Pronounced AH-KAY-OHS & AH-KAY-AHS)

aquellos hombres	[*those* men]	[m]
aquellas mujeres	[*those* women]	[f]

[6] The *Indefinite Articles* are also gendered, thus:

In English, the *singular* "a" or "an" (*a* moment, *an* apple)
are either "**un**" [m] or "**una**" [f], in Spanish,
depending on the gender of the noun:

un momento	(*a* moment)	[m]
una manzana	(*an* apple)	[f]

The English *plural* "some" (*some* moments, *some* apples) in Spanish
becomes "**unos**" or "**unas**", depending on the gender of the noun:

unos momentos	(*some* moments)	[m]
unas manzanas	(*some* apples)	[f]

The English plural "a few" (*a few* moments, *a few* apples)
in Spanish becomes "**algunos**" or "**algunas**",
depending on the gender of the noun:

(Pronounced ALL-GOO-NOSE & ALL-GOO-NAHS)

algunos momentos	(*a few* moments)	[m]
algunas manzanas	(*a few* apples)	[f]

Charles Mazal-Cami

For quick reference, here's the list:

Definitive Articles:

el	[m, singular]	**the**
la	[f, singular]	**the**
los	[m, plural]	**the**
las	[f, plural]	**the**
este	[m, singular]	**this**
esta	[f, singular]	**this**
ese	[m, singular]	**that**
esa	[f, singular]	**that**
estos	[m, plural]	**these**
estas	[f, plural]	**these**
esos	[m, plural]	**those**
esas	[f, plural]	**those**
aquellos	[m, plural]	**those**
aquellas	[f, plural]	**those**

Indefinite Articles:

un	[m, singular]	**a, an**
una	[f, singular]	**a, an**
unos	[m, plural]	**some**
unas	[f, plural]	**some**
algunos	[m, plural]	**a few**
algunas	[f, plural]	**a few**

ADJECTIVES ARE *ALSO* SEXY!

An adjective changes gender in accordance with the noun it modifies.

Remember that, in Spanish, the adjective comes *after* the noun!

El hombre astut**o** [m].....(The astute man)   [m, sing.]
La mujer astut**a** [f].......(The astute woman)   [f, sing.]

The adjective becomes plural if the noun is plural:

Los hombre**s** astut**os** .(The astute men)   [m, plural]
Las mujere**s** astut**as** ...(The astute women)   [f, plural]

If the adjective modifies masculine __and__ feminine nouns, use the masculine plural adjective:

Los hombre**s** y **las** mujere**s** astut**os**.......... (The astute men and women)
also
Las mujere**s** y **los** hombre**s** astut**os**.......... (The astute women and men)

Adjectives that end in "**e**", such as "Grand**e**" [large, or big],
do *not* change:

El hombre grand**e**   [The large man]
La mujer grand**e**   [The large woman]

Grande, incidentally, is also used in Spanish to describe an elderly person, which is more polite and sensitive than using the adjective "Viejo" [old]. In these cases, one would use the adjective in conjunction with the intransitive verb **"está"** [is], that denotes a state of being. i.e.:

El hombre *está* grande   [The man *is* old]
La mujer *está* grande   [The woman *is* old]
El hombre *está* contento   [The man is happy]
La mujer *está* contenta   [The woman *is* happy]

The intransitive *verb* "es**tá**" has an accent on the second syllable,
whereas the *article* "**es**ta" has *stress* on the first.

CHAPTER EIGHTEEN

CONJUGATING A VERB

The verb in Spanish *changes* when it is conjugated. In English, the verb remains substantially the same. Because of this, English is a relatively simple language to learn to *speak*, albeit in a primitive sort of way. Primitive, or "pidgin", English is spoken widely throughout the world because, once a verb is learned, it can be easily conjugated with little or no modification. However, *writing* and *reading* English is a different matter altogether!   Let's look at an example:

English	*Spanish*	
run	**correr** *[to Run]*	
I run	Yo corro	
You run	Tu corr**es**	
He run<u>s</u>	El corre	
She run<u>s</u>	Ella corre	[f]
We run	Nosotros corr**emos**	
They run	Ellos corr**en**	[m]
	Ellas corr**en**	[f]

Horrors!, you say. How could anyone *ever* learn the language?!
You were probably thinking the very same thing before you picked up
this book, and now....well, let's take a look:

In the above example, you will see that we have modified the verb
ending. The verb "corr<u>er</u>" *ends* in **...er**, and *all* verbs with that ending
would be modified (conjugated) the very same way.
In Spanish there are only *three* different verb endings.
[In English there are dozens!]

Let's extract a verb from one of the Rules we've learned. In Chapter Three we learned that English words ending in ....ate are translated to Spanish by *substituting* with ....ar.

Let's try **Elev<u>ate</u>**.

We know that, in Spanish, it's Elev**ar**. [*to* Elevate]

To conjugate this verb in Spanish, we will modify the *ending* (**...ar**) thus:

Yo elev**o**   (I elevate)
Tu elev**as**   (You elevate)
El elev**a**   (He elevates)
Ella elev**a**   [f]   (She elevates)
Nosotros elev**amos**   (We elevate)
Ellos elev**an**   (They elevate)
Ellas elev**an**   [f]   (They elevate)

You might want to try a conjugation on your own.

How about the verb **Don<u>ate</u>**?

Yo _____   (I donate)
Tu _____   (You donate)
El _____   (He donates)
Ella _____   (She donates) [f]
Nosotros _____   (We donate)
Ellos _____   (They donate)
Ellas _____   (They donate) [f]

Espectacular!
(Minor Rule # 1, Quirk # 6)

You have just created your first SENTENCES in Spanish!
(Not very *long* sentences, surely, but you have to begin *somewhere!*)

Spanish is a POLITE Language.

When referring to you, the *familiar* form in Spanish is **tu**.
However, if I don't know you very well, I will refer to you as
usted.

This is called the *polite* form.
(pronounced OOS-TE<u>TH</u> , soft "th" sound as in <u>TH</u>ey)

Usted can be abbreviated as **Ud.**, always with a capital "U".

If I am addressing a GROUP of people (the English plural is also "you")
usted becomes usted**es.**

The abbreviation for ustedes, is **Uds.**, with a capital "U".

The abbreviated forms (of course) are used only in *written* Spanish.

To conjugate the verb **elevar** using **usted** it looks like this:

Usted eleva   (You elevate -singular)
Ustedes elev**an**   (You elevate -plural)

Usted is *Neuter*, which means it can be used for **either**
Masculine **or** *Feminine* subjects.

Why not add these to *your* conjugation of the verb Don<u>ate</u>?
(*Spanish* Don<u>ar</u>)

Usted_____   (You donate)   [singular, Polite]
Ustedes _____   (You donate)   [plural, Polite]

Terrific!
(See Chapter Six to translate "Terrific" into Spanish)

Although it is a bit tiresome to remember all of this, it *does* have its advantages. Let's go back to the verb run and we'll learn a shortcut.

It's true that in English the conjugation is simple, but we must always attach the subject to the verb, as in *I* run, or *We* run.

In Spanish we modify the verb by changing its ending
(Yo corr*o*, Nosotros corr*emos)*.

By saying Corr*o*, we *imply* that it is I who runs.

By saying Corr*emos*, we *imply* that it is we who run.

Therefore, we can effectively *eliminate* the subject from the sentence by the treatment of the verb ending. We can state, simply:

(Yo)	Corr**o**	(I run)
(Tu)	Corr**es**	(You run)
(El)	Corr**e**	(He runs)
(Ella)	Corr**e**	(She runs)
(Usted)	Corr**e**	(You run) polite
(Nosotros)	Corr**emos**	(We run)
(Ellos)	Corr**en**	(They run)
(Ustedes)	Corr**en**	(You run) plural, polite

Of course, if the subject is feminine (ladies, for example) and we want to get the point across that "they" refers *specifically* to a group of lady joggers, we would say "*Ellas* corren". We would attach the subject only if we wanted to *specify* the gender of the subject, male *or* female.

There are only three verb *endings* in Spanish:

....ar   imitar [*to* imitate]

....er   comer [*to* eat]

...ir   sufrir [*to* suffer]

To conjugate verbs ending in **...ar,** as in the Spanish verb **imitar**
[*to* imitate], we *substitute* the ending with:

....o	for	(Yo) imit**o**	[I imitate]
....as	for	(Tu) imit**as**	[You imitate]
....a	for	(El) imit**a**	[He imitates]
	and	(Ella) imit**a**	[She imitates]
	and	(Usted) imit**a** [polite, singular]	[You imitate]
....an	for	(Ellos) imit**an**	[They imitate]
	and	(Ustedes) imit**an** [plural]	[You imitate]
....amos	for	(Nosotros) imit**amos**	[We imitate]

To conjugate verbs ending in **....er,** as in the Spanish verb **comer**
[*to* eat]), we *substitute* the ending with:

....o	for	(Yo) com**o**	[I eat]
....es	for	(Tu) com**es**	[You eat]
....e	for	(El) com**e**	[He eats]
	and	(Ella) com**e**	[She eats]
	and	(Usted) com**e** [polite, singular]	[You eat]
....en	for	(Ellos) com**en**	[They eat]
	and	(Ustedes) com**en** [plural]	[You eat]
....emos	for	(Nosotros) com**emos**	[We eat]

To conjugate verbs ending with **....ir**, (as in the Spanish verb **sufrir** [*to* suffer], we *substitute* the ending with:

....o	for	(Yo) súfro		[I suffer]
....es	for	(Tu) súfres		[You suffer]
....e	for	(El) súfre		[He suffers]
	and	(Ella) súfre		[She suffers]
	and	(Usted) súfre	[polite, singular]	[You suffer]
....en	for	(Ellos) súfren		[They suffer]
	and	(Ustedes) súfren	[plural]	[You suffer]
...imos	for	(Nosotros) sufrímos		[We suffer]

That pretty well covers the PRESENT tense.

Most of the Spanish *verbs* that you have learned in the previous Chapters (Three & Four) *end* in **...ar**, so at this point you should be able to conjugate nearly two thousand different Spanish verbs, depending on your command of *English!* In the Appendix, you will find many more verbs, with all *three* endings.

If you add a few thousand nouns, adjectives and adverbs, you can see that *you are well on your way to expressing yourself in Spanish!*

Don't forget that the subject (Yo, Tu, El, etc.) does not *need* to be included, except in cases where you want to *specify* that the subject is masculine *or* feminine or you are using the polite form (Usted),
in which case it is optional
(when you want to *specify* that you are being polite).

Let's take a look now at the

PAST TENSE

We will use the same verbs as we used in the Present Tense,
"imit**ar**" [to imitate], "com**er**" [to eat] and "suf**rir**" [to suffer]
for a clearer illustration:

For verbs ending in **...ar** we subsitute the ending with:

....é	for	(Yo) imit**é**	[I imitated]
....áste	for	(Tu) imit**áste**	[You imitated]
....ó	for	(El) imit**ó**	[He imitated]
	and	(Ella) imit**ó** [f]	[She imitated]
	and	(Usted) imit**ó** [polite. singular]	[You imitated]
....áron	for	(Ellos) imit**áron**	[They imitated]
	and	(Ellas) imit**áron** [f]	[They imitated]
	and	(Ustedes) imit**áron** [plural]	[You imitated]
....ámos	for	(Nosotros) imit**ámos**	[We imitated]

For verbs ending in **....er** we substitute the ending with:

....í	for	(Yo) com**í**	[I ate]
....íste	for	(Tu) com**íste**	[You ate]
....ió	for	(El) com**ió**	[He ate]
	and	(Ella) com**ió** [f]	[She ate]
	and	(Usted) com**ió** [polite, singular]	[You ate]
....iéron	for	(Ellos) com**iéron**	[They ate]
	and	(Ellas) com**iéron** [f]	[They ate]
	and	(Ustedes) com**iéron** [plural]	[You ate]
....ímos	for	(Nosostros) com**ímos**	[We ate]

For verbs ending in **....ir**, we substitute the ending with:

....í	for	(Yo) sufr**í**		[I suffered]
....íste	for	(Tu) sufr**íste**		[You suffered]
...ió	for	(El) sufr**ió**		[He suffered]
	and	(Ella) sufr**ió**	[f]	[She suffered]
	and	(Usted) sufr**ió**	[polite, singular]	[You suffered]
....iéron	for	(Ellos) sufr**iéron**		[They suffered]
	and	(Ellas) sufr**iéron**	[f]	[They suffered]
	and	(Ustedes) sufr**iéron**	[plural]	[You suffered]
....ímos	for	(Nosotros) sufr**ímos**		[We suffered]

Finally, with the same verbs, let's look at the

FUTURE TENSE

For verbs ending in **...ar**, we *add* the following *to* the ending:

....é	for	(Yo) imitar**é**		[I will imitate]
....ás	for	(Tu) imitar**ás**		[You will imitate]
....á	for	(El) imitar**á**		[He will imitate]
	and	(Ella) imitar**á**		[She will imitate]
	and	(Usted) imitar**á**	[polite]	[You will imitate]
....án	for	(Ellos) imitar**án**		[They will imitate]
	and	(Ellas) imitar**án**	[f]	[They will imitate]
	and	(Ustedes) imitar**án**	[plural]	[You will imitate]
....émos	for	(Nosotros) imitar**émos**		[We will imitate]

For verbs ending in **...er** we *add* the following *to* the ending:

....é	for	(Yo) comeré		[I will eat]
....ás	for	(Tu) comerás		[You will eat]
....á	for	(El) comerá		[He will eat]
	and	(Ella) comerá		[She will eat]
	and	(Usted) comerá	[polite, singular]	[You will eat]
....án	for	(Ellos) comerán		[They will eat]
	and	(Ellas) comerán	[f]	[They will eat]
	and	(Ustedes) comerán	[plural]	[You will eat]
....émos	for	(Nosotros) comerémos		[We will eat]

For verbs ending in ....**ir** we *add* the following *to* the ending:

....é	for	(Yo) sufriré		[I will suffer]
....ás	for	(Tu) sufrirás		[You will suffer]
....á	for	(El) sufrirá		[He will suffer]
	and	(Ella) sufrirá		[She will suffer]
	and	(Usted) sufrirá	[polite, singular]	[You will suffer]
....án	for	(Ellos) sufrirán		[They will suffer]
	and	(Ellas) sufrirán	[f]	[They will suffer]
	and	(Ustedes) sufrirán	[pl.]	[You will suffer]
....émos	for	(Nosotros) sufrirémos		[We will suffer]

Once again, remember that by saying **sufriré**, we are implying that it is *I* who *will* suffer. We need not attach the subject [yo] to get the meaning across. This, naturally, is true for *all* the verb tenses!

There are *other* tenses, of course, such as past-perfect, future-perfect, etc., that you will want to include in further studies. For the purposes of *this* book, however, we've covered the ground!
Felicitaciones* on having come this far!

This really isn't as frightening as it might appear. Go over this Chapter again and you will see that there is a logical sequence to Spanish verb conjugations. Spanish is very much like the Metric System, in that it follows a systematic pattern. In the Metric System, everything (both weights and measures) correlate to the same standard. The English language, on the other hand, like the British weights and measures, is haphazard and requires learning every word, weight and measurement individually! How long was the King's foot? How much does a hundred-weight weigh? Why is the letter K silent when followed by an N? How heavy was the stone? What happened to the P, G and H in phlegm? What is the volume of a quart? Where did the P go in Pneumonia? Why is a liquid ounce different from a solid ounce? And on, and on....it's madness, obviously.

Take a quick look at the Metric System:

> One cubic centimeter of water weighs one gram.
> One hundred centimeters measures one meter.
> One thousand grams weighs one kilogram.
> One thousand kilograms weighs one metric ton.
> One metric ton measures one cubic meter of water.

> Both weights *and* measures derive from the same, single source!

*See "Bad News" on Page 17

CHAPTER NINETEEN

SER & ESTAR

The verb "to be" in Spanish must have been thought up by a brilliantly tangled mind, both fool and genius, and is one of the stumbling blocks in Spanish. It isn't much better in English, either, with "to be" , "am", "is" and "are" all jockeying for position!

It is one of perhaps ten important radically-changing verbs in the Spanish language (English has its share, also).

Both **ser** and **estar** mean **"to be"**, although they cannot be used interchangeably without altering the meaning of the sentence.

Let's look, first, at the verb **ser** (to be).

The conjugation is as follows:

Spanish		*English*	
(Yo) **soy**	....	I am	
(Tu) **eres**	....	You are	
(El) **es**	....	He is	
(Ella) **es**	....	She is	
(Usted) **es**	....	You are	[Polite]
(Ellos) **son**	....	They are	
(Ellas) **son**	....	They are	[f]
(Ustedes) **son**	....	You are	[Plural]
(Nosotros) **somos**	....	We are	

As we have learned in previous Chapters, the *subject* does not need to be included. **"Soy"**, for example, *implies* that "*I* am".

The verb denotes something essential or expresses a characteristic about a person or thing :

(Yo) **soy** creativo	I *am* creative
(Tu) **eres** creativo............	You *are* creative
(El) **es** creativo.................	He *is* creative
(Ella) **es** creativa...............	She *is* creative
(Usted) **es** creativo............	You *are* creative [Polite]
(Ellos) **son** creativos.........	They *are* creative
(Ellas) **son** creativas..........	They *are* creative [f]
(Ustedes) **son** creativos.....	They are creative [Polite]
(Nosotros) **somos** creativos	We *are* creative

The verb **"estar"** [*to be*] is used mostly to denote
a subject's location, condition or position,
relative to some*thing* or some*place:*

(Yo) **estoy** aquí....................	I *am* here
(Tu) **estás** aquí....................	You *are* here
(El) **está** aquí......................	He *is* here
(Ella) **está** aquí..................	She *is* here [f]
(Usted) **está** aquí...............	You *are* here [Polite]
(Ellos) **están** aquí..............	They *are* here
(Ellas) **están** aquí..............	They *are* here [f]
(Ustedes) **están** aquí...........	You *are* here [Plural]
(Nosotros) **estámos** aquí......	We *are* here

This fairly covers the usage of this odd verb. You will learn to recognize the proper usage and inuendos as you explore the language further. In the above example, you will note that *está* is accentuated on the last syllable. This differentiates the verb from the article "esta" [f], wherein the emphasis (*stress*) is on the first syllable: *ES*-TA [see Chapter Seventeen]. The importance of the accent becomes obvious when differentiating between words that are similarly spelled.

Consider the following:

When using the Article **es**ta and the verb es**tá** in the same sentence, it would look like this:

este señor es**tá** aquí....   [this gentleman *is* here]
esta señora es**tá** aquí..   [this lady *is* here]

Señor and Señora are the *polite* designations for gentleman and lady, similar to "Sir" and "Madam", or "Mister" (Mr.) and "Mrs." in English. They are abbreviated Sr. (Señor) , and Sra. (Señora).

DIMINUTIVE & AUGMENTATIVE NOUNS

In Spanish, you don't need an adjective to make a noun "tiny".
You simply add a suffix!
(Called the "Diminutive form")

There's **...ita** for femenine-gendered nouns [f]
and **...ito** for masculine-gendered nouns [m]

"La casa" [f] (The house) becomes
"La cas**ita**" (The tiny house)

"El perro" [m] (The dog) becomes
"El per**rito**" (The tiny dog)

Attaching **...ita** [f] to Señora (Lady, or Mrs.) converts it to
"Señor**ita**" (*little* Lady, or Miss) !

The abbreviation for Señorita is "Srta."

There is no accepted word in Spanish for "Ms", although the
slang "Seño" is often used.

You can also make a noun **LARGE** with a Suffix
(Called the "Augmentative form")

There's **...óta** for femenine-gendered nouns [f]
and **...óte** for masculine-gendered nouns [m]

"La casóta" (the *big* house)

and

"El perróte" (the *big* dog)

The possibilities are endless!

Spanish, as you've seen, can be fun....and simple!

CHAPTER TWENTY

ROUNDUP

Of course there is a lot more to Spanish than we have covered in this book. But just think for a moment: when you began reading this book, you probably didn't know *any Spanish at all!*

We did not need to enter a lot of grammatical jargon to reach this point in the book. It is *precisely* that tedious process that discourages most people from learning a new language.

The many word examples set forth in the book are really not part of our learning process here, since you already *knew* the words in English. You had only to learn the *Rules* that apply to different English-word endings. Simple mathematics will tell you that by learning *fourteen Major* Rules, you learned approximately twenty thousand words in Spanish, an average of nearly fifteen *hundred* words for each Major Rule! To comply with the Title of this book, you will have had nearly one and three-quarters minutes to learn each of the one-word Major Rules, a time which was arrived at by sample testing and that, for some, might seem a bit ambitious.

Additionally, with the twenty-four *Minor* Rules, you learned another five thousand words, approximately, which is still nearly two-hundred words per *Minor* Rule on the average! These averages, naturally, will vary in accordance with your own command of the *English* language, which took you, very likely, *years* to learn!

Whatever the case, *you have learned thousands of words in Spanish, you know what they mean, you know how to read and write them, you know how to pronounce them and you will likely never forget them* (unless you forget how to speak English!).

Beyond that, (although not part of the Twenty Minutes) you have *also* learned how to *recognize word genders,* how to *conjugate verbs* and how to search for verbs, nouns, adverbs and adjectives among the Rules we've covered.

That is sufficient reason to give yourself a pat on the back!

If you travel to a Spanish-speaking country *after* having read this book, it will amaze you how much you *do* understand, and it should make you curious to learn what you don't *yet* understand. People in Latin America really don't *expect* you to know their language but they are pleased and flattered if you at least *try*. What you have learned in this book will allow you to make the effort and still feel confident that you know the *meaning* of what you are saying. After all, if you know what a word means in English, and you have now learned how to translate it to Spanish, then you know precisely what it is you are talking about!

In the following *Appendix*, you will find hundreds of identical (and nearly identical) English-Spanish words, including hundreds of verbs, in *addition* to those we have already covered in the Rules. These *"Matching Words"* are meant to further stimulate your desire to speak and study Spanish and to demonstrate that the chasm between English and Spanish is not nearly so wide as you might have thought.

Also in the Appendix, there is a condensed dictionary of practical phrases for the traveler, common usage nouns including those that describe food, office equipment, animals, furniture, services and even insects! There are additional useful verbs (and their conjugations) as well as Spanish translations for colors, shapes and textures and you will even find longhand numbers (so that you can write a check in Spanish). And, on the final page of the Appendix, you'll find a *Cheat Sheet* that shows all of the Major & Minor Rules - a handy quick reference! (If you're a student, *please* don't take the "cheat sheet" along to the classroom during exams!)

Charles Mazal-Cami

Pronunciation is the key to learning more of the language, so be sure to read and re-read the first Chapter! *Practice out loud, often!* Don't be shy! Many people who have studied two or more years of Spanish in high-school very likely know (or remember) only a *fraction* of the Spanish words you have just learned! *More* than likely, they would not be able to tell you what the Spanish translations for *Superconductive* or *Coefficient* or *Anachronism* are!

You can now practice your pronunciation on *any* Spanish word, whether or not we've covered it in this book. If you have made an honest effort in learning the First Chapter, you will know that

Hasta is pronounced AHS-TAH, and
luego is pronounced LOO-EH-GO

which in Spanish isn't quite "Good-bye". It literally means "Until later", and is the Spanish equivalent of SO LONG!

Food for thought...

Have you ever wondered why you cannot consciously recall events in your life that took place *before* you could understand words? Surely, there were many important events, not the least of which was the moment of birth, and yet these events *seem* to have evaporated from your life. The images *must* be there, somewhere, but somehow you are not able to retrieve them from your memory bank! Your earliest recollections are sketchy and incomplete, in tune, you might say, with the extent of your vocabulary at the time. It seems that the mind is a storage house of images for which *words* are the keys to their retrieval. If so, then words are far more than just sounds that we use to express ourselves or understand the thoughts of others. They are also the very flags which our mind uses to label each and every file of images and experiences. One might conclude that by learning more words we could expand our ability to store more *retrievable* images and knowledge. What we *know*, basically, is what we can consciously *retrieve*. Is it fair, then, to say that by expanding our vocabulary we are simultaneously expanding our ability to retrieve stored knowledge?

Charles Mazal-Cami

Appendix

Matching Words

The principle object of this book is to encourage you to learn more Spanish by demonstrating the striking similarities between English and Spanish. Yes, you **CAN** (and at this point in the book, **DO**) *SPEAK SPANISH!*

"Matching Words" should dissipate any remaining fears that you might have about learning Spanish. You are not expected, of course, to *memorize* each of these translations, but the sheer number of *similar* English-Spanish words that are listed here further exemplifies that Spanish is **not** the obscure and difficult language you might have thought it to be before you read this book!

In ***addition*** to the words you have already learned in the preceding Chapters, many of which are *spelled identically in English and in Spanish* (such as the **...AL, ...AR, ...BLE, ...OR** and **...SION** Rules), here is a curious listing of Matching Words that ought to stimulate your curiosity! See how many more "Rules" *you* can discover!

Remember proper Spanish Pronunciation!
[See Chapter One]

Some of these words are designated [verb] after the Spanish translation. To conjugate these verbs, see Chapter Eighteen. You will also find here some of the exceptions to the above-indicated Rules [i.e. Amia**ble** in English is Ama**ble** in Spanish]. Where an English word has different meanings [i.e."Bulb"] these are indicated and translations for both meanings are provided.

There are 150 (count 'em!) new verbs listed here with all three endings (**..ar, ..er, ..ir**) to add to those that you have already learned!

English	Spanish Same Spelling	Spanish Slightly Different Spelling	Notes
Abacus		Abaco	
Abalone		Abulón	
Abandon		Abandonar	(verb)
Abandon		Abandono	(noun)
Abdomen	Abdomen		
Abnormal		Anormal	
Aborigines	Aborígenes		
Abort		Abortar	(verb)
Abortion		Aborto	
Abrazo		Abrazo	
Absolute		Absoluto	
Abstract		Abstracto	
Absurd		Absurdo	
Abundance		Abundancia	
Abundant		Abundante	
Academy		Academia	
Accord		Acorde	
Acetate		Acetato	
Acetone		Acetona	
Access		Acceso	
Accord		Acorde	
Accordion		Acordión	
Acid		Ácido	
Acrobat		Acróbata	
Adenoid		Adenoíde	
Adict		Adicto	
Adept		Adepto	
Adios	Adiós		
Admire		Admirar	(verb)
Admission		Admisión	
Admit		Admitir	(verb)
Adobe	Adobe		
Adopt		Adoptar	(verb)
Adorn		Adornar	(verb)
Adult		Adulto	
Advalorem	Advalorem		
Advance		Avanzar	(verb)
Adventure		Aventura	
Adverb		Adverbio	

English	Spanish Same Spelling	Spanish Slightly Different Spelling	Notes
Aerodrome		Aereodromo	
Aeroplane		Aereoplano	
Aero		Aéreo	
Aerosol		Aereosol	
Affect		Afectar	(verb)
Africa	África		
African		Africano	
Afro-	Afro-		
Algebra	Álgebra		[Quirk # 12!]
Agar	Agar		
Agate		Agato	
Aggressor		Agresor	
Agriculture		Agricultura	
Air		Aire	
Alamo	Álamo		
Alarm		Alarma	
Alaska	Alaska		
Albino	Albino		
Albumin		Albúmina	
Alcohol	Alcohol		
Alfalfa	Alfalfa		
Algae		Alga	
Algebra	Álgebra		
Alkali	Alkalí		
Alliance		Alianza	
Almanac	Almanac		
Alpaca	Alpaca		
Alpha		Alfa	
Alphabet		Alfabeto	
Alpine		Alpino	
Altar	Altar		
Alter		Alterar	(verb)
Altitude		Altitud	[also Altura]
Alto	Alto		
Alveolar	Alveolar		
Amalgam		Amalgama	
Amaretto		Amareto	
Amarillo	Amarillo		
Amateur	Amateur		

English	Spanish Same Spelling	Spanish Slightly Different Spelling	Notes
Amber		Ambar	
Ambient		Ambiente	
Ambrosia	Ambrosia		
Ambulance		Ambulancia	
Amiable		Amable	
Amicable		Amigable	
Amino	Amino		
Ammonia		Amoniaco	
Amnion	Amnión		
Amoeba		Ameba	
Ampere		Amper	
Amphora		Ánfora	
Amplitude		Amplitud	
Ampule		Ámpula	
Amulet		Amuleto	
Anaconda	Anaconda		
Analog		Análogo	
Analysis		Análisis	
Anarchy		Anarquía	
Anatomy		Anatomía	
Ancestor		Ancestro	
Anecdote		Anécdota	
Anemia	Anemia		
Anemone		Anemón	
Aneroid		Aneroide	
Anesthesia		Anestésia	
Angel	Angel		
Angelica	Angélica		
Angina	Angina		
Angostura	Angostura		
Anis	Anís		
Anisette		Anís	
Anode		Ánodo	
Anorexia	Anorexia		
Antecessor		Antecesor	
Antedeluvian		Antedeluviano	
Antemeridian		Antemeridiano	
Anticoagulant		Anticoagulante	
Antigen		Antígeno	

English	Spanish Same Spelling	Spanish Slightly Different Spelling	Notes
Aorta	Aorta		
Apache	Apache		
Apart		Aparte	
Apnea	Apnea		
Apostrophe		Apóstrofe	
Apart		Aparte	
Appetite		Apetito	
Aptitude		Aptitud	
Aqueduct		Acueducto	
Arab		Árabe	
Arc		Arco	
Architect		Arquitecto	
Archive		Archivo	
Argon	Argón		
Argument		Argumento	
Aristocrat		Aristócrata	
Arm [weapon]		Arma	
Armadillo	Armadillo		
Armament		Armamento	
Arrest		Arrestar	(verb)
Art		Arte	
Artery		Arteria	
Artist		Artista	
Asafetida	Asafétida		
Asbestos		Asbesto	
Aspect		Aspecto	
Aspire	Aspire	Aspirar	(verb)
Assist		Asiste	
Asterisk		Asterisco	
Asteroid		Asteroide	
Asthma		Asma	
Astral	Astral		
Astringent		Astringente	
Astronaut		Astronauta	
Astute		Astuto	Astuta [f]
Atlas	Atlas		
Atmosphere		Atmósfera	
Atom		Átomo	
Audio	Audio		

English	Spanish Same Spelling	Spanish Slightly Different Spelling	Notes
Audit		Auditar	(verb)
Auditor	Auditor		
Aura	Aura		
Auricular	Auricular		
Aurora	Aurora		
Austere		Austero	Austera [f]
Author		Autor	
Auto	Auto		
Autoclave	Autoclave		
Automobile		Automóvil	
Axis	Axis		also Eje
Bacteria	Bacteria		
Badminton	Badminton		
Baffle	Baffle		
Baklava	Báklava		
Balance	Balance		
Balance [the verb]		Balancear	(verb)
Ballad		Balada	
Ballast		Balasta	
Ballet	Ballet		
Balsam		Bálsamo	
Balsa	Balsa		
Bambino	Bambino		
Bamboo		Bambú	
Banana		Banano	
Bandana	Bandana		
Bank		Banco	
Barracuda	Barracuda		
Barrel		Barril	
Barricade		Barricada	
Baritone		Barítono	
Baron	Barón		
Basal	Basal		
Base	Base		
Basilica	Basílica		
Bastion	Bastión		
Baton	Batón		
Battery		Batería	
Begonia	Begonia		

English	Spanish Same Spelling	Spanish Slightly Different Spelling	Notes
Benefit		Beneficio	
Beta	Beta		
Bible		Biblia	
Bidet	Bidet		
Bicarbonate		Bicarbonato	
Bigamy		Bigamía	
Bikini	Bikini		
Biography		Biografia	
Boa	Boa		
Bomb		Bomba	
Bonanza	Bonanza		
Bongo	Bongó		
Bordello		Bordelo	
Brandy	Brandy		
Brassiere	Brassiere		[also Brasier]
Bravado	Bravado		
Bravo	Bravo		
Broccoli		Brócoli	
Brute		Bruto	
Buffet		Bufete	
Bulb (flower)		Bulbo	
Bulb (electronic)		Bulbo	
Cabaret	Cabaret		
Cabin		Cabina	
Cabriolet	Cabriolet		
Cacao	Cacao		
Cactus	Cactus		
Cadaver	Cadaver		
Cadet		Cadete	
Cafe	Café		
Calendar		Calendario	
Caliber		Calíbre	
Calico	Cálico		
Calm		Calma	
Calm [the verb]		Calmar	(verb)
Calorie		Caloría	
Camera		Cámara	
Camphor		Canfor	[also Alcanfor]
Canal	Canal		

English	Spanish Same Spelling	Spanish Slightly Different Spelling	Notes
Canape	Canapé		
Canasta	Canasta		
Cancel		Cancelar	(verb)
Cancer	Cáncer		
Candid		Cándido	
Candidate		Candidato	
Cannibal		Caníbalo	
Cannula		Cánula	
Capon	Capón		
Capsule		Cápsula	
Car		Carro	
Caravan		Caravana	
Carbon	Carbón		
Caricature		Caricatura	
Carnival		Carnaval	
Casino	Casino		
Caste		Casta	
Catalog		Catálogo	
Catamaran	Catamarán		
Catastrophe		Catástrofe	
Category		Categoría	
Cellulose		Celulosa	
Cement [the noun]		Cemento	
Cement [the verb]		Cementar	(verb)
Center [the noun]		Centro	
Center [the verb]		Centrar	(verb)
Centrifuge [the noun]		Centrífuga	
Centrifuge [the verb]		Centrifugar	(verb)
Chalet	Chalet		
Charlatan	Charlatán		
Character		Carácter	
Charisma		Carísma	
Chassis		Chasís	
Chef	Chef		
Chile	Chile		
Chili		Chile	
Chinchilla	Chinchilla		
Chocolate	Chocolate		
Cholesterol		Colesterol	

English	Spanish Same Spelling	Spanish Slightly Different Spelling	Notes
Chromosome		Cromosoma	
Cigarillo		Cigarrillo	
Cinema	Cinema		
Circa	Circa		
Circuit		Circuito	
Cistern		Cisterna	
Civil	Civil		
Clarinet		Clarinete	
Climate		Clima	
Climax	Clímax		
Clinic		Clínica	
Clitoris	Clítoris		
Closet	Closet		
Club	Club		
Cobalt		Cobalto	
Cobra	Cobra		
Cocaine		Cocaína	
Cocoa	Cocóa		
Colibri	Colibrí		
Colon	Colon		
Colorado	Colorado		
Column		Columna	
Coma	Coma		
Combat		Combate	(noun)
Combat		Combatir	(verb)
Combustion	Combustión		
Comedy		Comédia	
Comfort		Confort	
Compassion		Compasión	
Compact		Compacto	
Compass		Compás	
Concave		Cóncavo	
Condom		Condón	
Cone		Cono	
Confess		Confesar	(verb)
Confessor		Confesor	
Confetti		Confeti	
Conflict		Conflicto	
Congestion	Congestión		

English	Spanish Same Spelling	Spanish Slightly Different Spelling	Notes
Congress		Congreso	
Conservatory		Conservatorio	
Console		Consola	
Consonant		Consonante	
Conspire	Conspire	Conspirar	(verb)
Consul	Cónsul		
Consult		Consultar	(verb)
Consume		Consumir	(verb)
Contact		Contacto	
Contact		Contactar	(verb)
Content		Contento	
Contraband		Contrabando	
Contrast	Contraste (noun)		
Contrast		Contrastar	(verb)
Control	Control (noun)		
Control [the verb]		Controlar	(verb)
Convent		Convento	
Cordon	Cordón		
Corona	Corona		
Correct		Corregir	(verb)
Correct		Correcto	(adj.)
Correspond		Corresponder	(verb)
Corridor		Corredor	
Corrupt		Corrupto	
Cortex	Cortex		
Cosmos	Cosmos		
Coyote	Coyote		
Crater	Cráter		
Credit		Crédito	
Credit		Acreditar	(verb)
Crepe (paper)	Crepé		
Crepe (food)		Crepa	
Crest		Cresta	
Crisis	Crisis		
Crude		Crudo	
Crusade		Crusada	
Cube		Cubo	
Cuadruple	Cuádruple		
Cupula	Cúpula		

Charles Mazal-Cami

English	Spanish _Same Spelling_	Spanish _Slightly Different Spelling_	Notes
Cursor	Cursor		
Curve		Curva	
Dado	Dado		
Dahlia	Dahlia		
Daiquiri	Daiquirí		
Dame		Dama	
Dance		Danza	
Data	Data		
Debacle	Debacle		
Debate	Debate		(noun)
Debate		Debatir	(verb)
Debit		Débito	
Debut	Debut		
Debutante	Debutante		
Deca	Deca		
Decade		Década	
Decalcomonia		Calcomanía	
Decathlon		Decatlón	
Decorum	Decorum		
Decibel	Decibel		
Decide		Decidir	(verb)
Decline		Declinar	(verb)
Deduce		Deducir	(verb)
Defacto	Defacto		
Defame		Defamar	(verb)
Deficit	Déficit		
Define	Define	Definir	(verb)
Degrade		Degradar	(verb)
Delincuency		Delincuencia	
Delinquent		Delincuente	
Delirium		Delirio	
Delta	Delta		
Deluxe	Deluxe		
Demand		Demandar	(verb)
Demerit		Demérito	
Democrat		Demócrata	
Demon		Demónio	
Demure		Demura	
Denier	Denier		

English	Spanish Same Spelling	Spanish Slightly Different Spelling	Notes
Dense		Denso	
Dentist		Dentista	
Depend		Depender	(verb)
Dependency		Dependencia	
Deport		Deporta	
Deposit		Depósito	(noun)
Deposit		Depositar	(verb)
Derelict		Derelicto	
Dermatome		Dermatomo	
Describe		Describir	(verb)
Despot		Déspota	
Detective	Detective		
Determine		Determinar	(verb)
Detest		Detestar	(verb)
Detonator		Detonador	
Diabetes	Diabetes		
Diagram		Diagrama	
Dialect		Dialecto	
Dialogue		Diálogo	
Dialysis		Diálisis	
Diapason	Diapasón		
Diaphragm		Diafragma	
Diarrhea		Diarréa	
Diathermy		Diatermia	
Dictator		Dictador	
Dielectric		Dieléctrico	
Diesel	Diesel		
Diet		Dieta	(noun)
Diet [the verb]		*Estar* a Dieta	
Digit		Dígito	
Digitalis	Digitalis		
Dilemma		Dilema	
Dilute		Diluto	
Dilute [the verb]		Diluir	(verb)
Dinosaur		Dinosáuro	
Diode		Diodo	
Dioxide		Dióxido [also Bióxido]	
Diploma	Diploma		
Diplomat		Diplómata	

English	Spanish *Same Spelling*	Spanish *Slightly Different Spelling*	Notes
Direct		Directo	(adj.)
Direct		Dirigir	(verb)
Disc		Disco	
Discipline		Disciplina	
Disco	Disco		
Discontinue		Discontinuar	(verb)
Disgrace		Desgracia	
Disgrace		Desgraciar	(verb)
Disk		Disco	
Disorient		Desorientar	(verb)
Disperse		Dispersar	(verb)
Distance		Distancia	
Distil		Destilar	(verb)
Distinct		Distincto	
District		Distrito	
Divan	Diván		
Divide		Dividir	(verb)
Dividend		Dividendo	
Docile		Dócil	
Doctrine		Doctrina	
Document		Documento	(noun)
Document		Documentar	(verb)
Dogma	Dogma		
Dollar		Dólar	
Dome		Domo	
Domicile		Domicilio	
Domino	Dominó		
Dominion		Dominio	
Dorado	Dorado		
Dose		Dosis	
Dosis	Dosis		
Double		Doble	
Dragon	Dragón		
Drama	Drama		
Dual	Duál		
Ductile		Ductil	
Duet		Dueto	
Duo	Duo		
Duplex	Duplex		

English	Spanish Same Spelling	Spanish Slightly Different Spelling	Notes
Dura	Dura		
Echo		Eco	
Eclipse	Eclipse		
Ecstasy		Écstasis	
Ecuator		Ecuador	
Eczema		Ecsema	
Edema	Edema		
Edit		Editar	(verb)
Effect		Efecto	
Ego	Ego		
Electrocardiogram		Electrocardiograma	
Electrode		Electrodo	
Electron	Electrón		
Elegant		Elegante	
Elephant		Elefante	
Elevator		Elevador	
Elixir	Elíxir		
Ellipse		Elipse	
Embargo	Embargo		
Embargo [the verb]		Embargar	(verb)
Emblem		Emblema	
Embryo		Embrio	
Emergency		Emergencia	
Emerald		Esmeralda	
Emir	Emir		
Emit		Emitir	(verb)
Emphasis		Énfasis	
Encyclopedia		Enciclopedia	
Endocarditis	Endocarditis		
Endogen		Endógeno	
Energy		Energía	
Enigma	Enigma		
Enlace	Enlace		
Enthusiasm		Entusiasmo	
Enzyme		Enzima	
Epiglottis		Epiglotis	
Epilepsy		Epilepsia	
Episode		Episodio	
Epoch		Época	

English	Spanish Same Spelling	Spanish Slightly Different Spelling	Notes
Epoxy		Epóxido	
Equator		Ecuador	
Equestrian		Ecuestre	
Equilibrium		Equilibrio	
Equip		Equipar	(verb)
Equipment		Equipo	[also means Team]
Era	Era		
Err		Errar	(verb)
Errata	Errata		
Erotica	Erótica		
Escape	Escape		(noun)
Escape		Escapar	(verb)
Espresso		Expresso	
Essence		Esencia	
Estrus		Estro	
Etcetera	Etcétera		
Ether		Eter	
Eucaliptus		Eucalipto	
Eureka	Eureka		
Europe		Europa	
Evade		Evadir	(verb)
Event		Evento	
Exact		Exacto	
Examen	Examen		
Examine		Examinar	(verb)
Except		Excepto	
Excerpt		Excerpto	
Excess		Exceso	
Excuse		Escusa	(noun)
Excuse		Excusar	(verb)
Expand		Expander	(verb)
Export		Exportar	(verb)
Expose		Exponer	(verb)
Expositor	Expositor		
Exist		Existe	
Existent		Existente	
Experiment		Experimento	(noun)
Experiment		Experimentar	(verb)
External		Externo	

English	Spanish Same Spelling	Spanish Slightly Different Spelling	Notes
Extinct		Extincto	
Extra	Extra		
Extravaganza	Extravaganza		
Extreme		Extremo	
Exuberant		Exuberante	
Facet		Faceta	
Falcon	Falcón		
False		Falso	
Family		Familia	
Fantasm		Fantasma	
Fatigue		Fatiga	(noun)
Fatigue		Fatigar	(verb)
Fauna	Fauna		
Feminine		Femenino	
Femur	Fémur		
Ferment		Fermentar	(verb)
Fertile		Fértil	
Fetus		Feto	
Fibre (or Fiber)		Fibra	
Fibula	Fíbula		
Figure		Figura	(noun)
Figure		Figurar	(verb)
Filaria	Filaria		
Fillet		Filete	(noun)
Fillet		Filetear	(verb)
Filter		Filtro	(noun)
Filter		Filtrar	(verb)
Fin (end)	Fin		
Finance		Finanza	
Fine		Fino	(adj.)
Flamenco	Flamenco		
Flamingo	Flamingo		
Flora	Flora		
Florid		Flórido	
Flotilla	Flotilla		
Fluid		Fluido	
Fluorescence		Fluorescencia	
Fluothane		Fluotano	
Foliage	Foliage		

English	Spanish Same Spelling	Spanish Slightly Different Spelling	Notes
Folio	Folio		
Forage	Forage		
Forceps	Forceps		
Form	Forma		
Format		Formato	(noun)
Format		Formatear	(verb)
Formula	Fórmula		
Fortune		Fortuna	
Fossil		Fósil	
Fracture		Fractura	
Fracture [the verb]		Fracturar	(verb)
Fragile		Frágil	
Fragment		Fragmento	(noun)
Fragment		Fragmentar	(verb)
Fragrance		Fragancia	
Freon	Freón		
Frequency		Frecuencia	
Frigid		Frígido	
Frijol	Frijol		
Fronton	Frontón		
Fruit		Fruta	
Fumarole		Fumarola	
Future		Futuro	
Gabardine		Gabardina	
Gala	Gala		
Galaxy		Galaxia	
Galleon		Galeón	
Gallon		Galón	
Galleria		Galeria	
Gamma		Gama	
Gangrene		Gangrena	
Garage	Garage		
Garrote	Garrote		
Gas	Gas		
Gelatin		Gelatina	
Gendarme	Gendarme		
Genesis	Génesis		
Genitalia	Genitalia		
Genius		Genio	

English	Spanish Same Spelling	Spanish Slightly Different Spelling	Notes
Genuine		Genuino	
Germicide		Germicida	
Gigolo	Gígolo		
Globule		Glóbulo	
Glory		Gloria	
Glutton		Glotón	
Glycerine		Glicerina	
Golf	Golf		
Gondola	Góndola		
Gorrila		Gorila	
Gram		Gramo	
Grand		Grande	
Gratis	Gratis		
Grave (the adjective)	Grave		
Guard		Guardia	(noun)
Guard		Guardar	(verb)
Guardian	Guardián		
Guru	Gurú		
Gymnast		Gimnasta	
Habeas corpus	Habeas corpus		
Habitant		Habitante	
Harmony		Harmonía	
Harpoon		Harpón	
Hectare		Hectárea	
Helicoid		Helicoidal	
Helicopter		Helicóptero	
Helix	Hélix		
Hematocrit		Hematocrito	
Hemorhage		Hemorrágia	
Hemorhoid		Hemorroide	
Heparin		Heparina	
Herald		Heraldo	
Herb		Hierba	
Herbal		Hierbal	
Hero		Héroe	
Hexagon		Hexágono	
Hippopotamus		Hipopótamo	
History		Historia	
Homeopath		Homeópata	

English	Spanish Same Spelling	Spanish Slightly Different Spelling	Notes
Homicide		Homicida	
Horizon		Horizonte	
Hostile		Hostil	
Human		Humano	
Hybrid		Híbrido	
Hydrocortisone		Hidrocortisona	
Hydrogen		Hidrógeno	
Hypnosis		Hipnosis	
Hypocrite		Hipócrita	
Idiom		Idioma	
Idiot		Idiota	
Idol		Ídolo	
Ignorance		Ignorancia	
Iguana	Iguana		
Illicit		Ilícito	
Image		Imagen	
Immobile		Inmovil	
Impact		Impacto	(noun)
Impact		Impactar	(verb)
Impediment		Impedimento	
Impetigo	Impétigo		
Implant		Implante	(noun)
Implant		Implantar	(verb)
Implement		Implementar	(verb)
Importance		Importancia	
Impulse		Impulso	
Incision	Incisión		
Incisor	Incisor		
Incongnito	Incógnito		
Indecorum	Indecorum		
Indigo	Indigo		
Inert		Inerte	
Inertia		Inercia	
Infantile		Infantil	
Infect		Infectar	(verb)
Infidel	Infidel		
Influence		Influencia	
Influenza	Influenza		
Inform		Informar	(verb)

English	Spanish Same Spelling	Spanish Slightly Different Spelling	Notes
Informant		Informante	
Innuendo		Inuendo	
Insomnia	Insomnia		
Instant		Instante	
Insulin		Insulina	
Intellect		Intelecto	
Intense		Intenso	
Interest		Interés	
Intercept		Interceptar	(verb)
Interferon	Interferón		
Intermediary		Intermediario	
Intermezzo	Intermezzo		
Intern [noun]		Interno	
Intern [the verb]		Internar	(verb)
Internal		Interno	
Interpol	Interpol		
Interval		Intervalo	
Intestine		Intestino	
Intrauterine		Intrauterino	
Introduce		Introducir	(verb)
Invalid		Inválido	
Invent		Inventar	(verb)
Ion	Ión		
Iris	Iris		
Isle		Isla	
Israel	Israel		
Israeli	Israelí		
Italian		Italiano	
Italix	Italix		
Jacaranda	Jacaranda		
Jaguar	Jaguar		
Jai-alai	Jai-alai		
Jalisco	Jalisco		
Jamaica	Jamaica		
Jesus	Jesús		
Jubilant		Jubilante	
Judas	Judas		
Jugular		Yugular	
July		Julio	

English	Spanish Same Spelling	Spanish Slightly Different Spelling	Notes
June		Junio	
Jupiter	Júpiter		
Just		Justo	
Kangaroo		Kanguro [also Canguro]	
Karate	Karate		
Karma	Karma		
Keratosis	Keratosis		
Kerosene		Kerosina	
Kibbutz		Kibutz	
Kilo	Kilo		
Kilogram		Kilogramo	
Kiwi	Kiwi		
Kleptomania	Kleptomanía		
Korea	Koréa		
Kosher	Kosher		
Kudu	Kudú		
Lactase	Lactase		
Lactobacillus		Lactobacilo	
Lactose		Lactosa	
Lagoon		Laguna	
Lament		Lamento	(noun)
Lament		Lamentar	(verb)
Lamina	Lámina		
Language		Lenguaje [also Idioma]	
Lapse		Lapso	
Larva	Larva		
Lasagna	Lasagna [pron. "Lasaña"]		
Laser	Láser		
Latex	Látex		
Laurel	Laurel		
Lava	Lava		
Lecture		Lectura	(noun)
Legislature		Legislatura	
Lemon		Limón	
Leukemia	Leukemia		
Liberty		Libertad	
Libra	Libra		
License		Licencia	
Limbo	Limbo		

English	Spanish Same Spelling	Spanish Slightly Different Spelling	Notes
Lime		Lima	
Lime		Limón	
Limousine		Limosina	
Linguist		Linguista	
Lipid		Lípido	
Liquid		Líquido	
Lira	Lira		
Llama	Llama		
Loran	Lorán		
Lottery		Lotería	
Lotus	Lotus		
Lubricator		Lubricador	
Lumbar	Lumbar		
Lumen	Lumen		
Lunar	Lunar		
Lupus		Lupo	
Lustre		Lustro	
Lux	Lux		
Luxuriant		Lujuriante	
Luxurious		Lujoso	
Macabre		Macabro	
Macaroon		Macarrón	
Machete	Machete		
Macro	Macro		
Maduro	Maduro		
Maestro	Maestro		
Magazine	Magazine		[also Revista]
Magma	Magma		
Magneto	Magneto		
Magnetron	Magnetrón		
Magnifico	Magnífico		
Magnificent		Magnífico	
Magnolia	Magnolia		
Maguey	Maguey		
Maharajah		Majaraya	
Maharani		Majarani	
Maize		Maiz	
Major		Mayor	
Major (rank)		Mayor	

English	Spanish Same Spelling	Spanish Slightly Different Spelling	Notes
Malaria	Malaria		
Malta	Malta		
Mamba	Mamba		
Mambo	Mambo		
Mamma		Mamá	
Mañana	Mañana		
Mana	Maná		
Manatee		Manatí	
Mandrill		Mandril	
Mango	Mango		
Mania	Manía		
Manicure	Manicure		
Manifest		Manifesto	(noun)
Manifest		Manifestar	(verb)
Manifesto	Manifesto		
Manila	Manila		
Manipular	Manipular		
Manta	Manta		
Mantilla	Mantilla		
Map		Mapa	
Maple	Maple		
Maraca	Maraca		
Marathon		Maratón	
Margarita	Margarita		
Margin		Margen	
Marimba	Marimba		
Marina	Marina		
Marine (deck hand)		Marinero	
Marlin	Marlin		
Marmalade		Mermelada	
Marroon		Marrón	
Martini	Martini		
Martyr		Martir	
Mascot		Mascota	
Mason	Masón		
Mass (physical)		Masa	
Mass (religious cerem.)		Misa	
Massacre		Masacre	
Massage		Masaje	

English	Spanish Same Spelling	Spanish Slightly Different Spelling	Notes
Masseur		Maseur	
Mastic		Mastique	
Mastodon		Mastondonte	
Mastoid		Mastoide	
Mate (as in Chess)	Mate		
Matrix		Matriz	
Matte		Mate	
Matter (noun)		Materia	
Mausoleum		Mausoleo	
Maxilla		Maxila	
Maximum		Máximo	
Mayonaise		Mayonesa	
Medalist		Medalista	
Media		Medio	
Medicine		Medicina	
Megalopolis	Megalópolis		
Melancholia		Melancolía	
Melodica	Melódica		
Melody		Melodía	
Melon	Melón		
Membrane		Membrana	
Memento	Memento		
Memory		Memoria	
Menace		Amenaza	
Meniscus		Menisco	
Menthol		Mentol	
Menu	Menú		
Mercury		Mercurio	
Meridian		Meridiano	
Merino	Merino		
Mesa (geology)	Mesa [means table]	Meseta [geology]	
Mescaline		Mescalina	
Mesquite		Mezquite	
Messiah		Mesias	
Metamorphosis		Metamórfosis	
Metastasis	Metástasis		
Metatarsus		Metatarso	
Meteor		Meteoro	
Meter (also Metre)		Metro	

English	Spanish Same Spelling	Spanish Slightly Different Spelling	Notes
Methane		Metano	
Methanol		Metanol	
Method		Método	
Methodist		Metodista	
Methyl		Metil	
Metro	Metro		
Metronome		Metrónomo	
Metropolis	Metrópolis		
Metropolitan		Metropolitano	
Mezzanine		Mezanine	
Mica	Mica		
Micro	Micro		
Microbe		Microbio	
Microparasite		Microparásito	
Microprocessor		Microporocesador	
Midi (prefix)	Midi		
Mil	Mil		(means "thousand")
Militia		Milicia	
Million		Millón	
Mimosa	Mimosa		
Mini (prefix)	Mini		
Miniature		Miniatura	
Minima	Mínima		
Minister		Ministrar	(verb)
Minister		Ministro	(noun)
Minor		Menor	
Minuet		Minueto	
Miscelanea		Miscelania	
Misery		Miseria	
Missile		Misil	
Mission		Misión	
Mobile		Móvil	
Mode		Modo	
Model		Modelo	
Modem	Módem		
Modern		Moderno	
Modest		Modesto	
Modesty		Modestia	
Mollecule		Molécula	

English	Spanish Same Spelling	Spanish Slightly Different Spelling	Notes
Molest		Molestar	(verb)
Monarch		Monarca	
Mongol	Mongol		
Mongolia	Mongolia		
Monochrome		Monocromo	
Monomania	Monomanía		
Monopoly		Monopolio	
Monte	Monte		
Monterrey	Monterrey		
Morbid		Mórbido	
Morgue	Morgue		
Mortar		Mortero	
Mosquito	Mosquito		
Much		Mucho	
Mucus		Mucosa	
Mule		Mula	
Multi (prefix)	Multi		
Multiple	Múltiple		
Multitude		Multitud	
Mundane		Mundano	
Murmur		Murmuro	
Mutant		Mutante	
Mutual		Mutuo	
Mystery		Misterio	
Naptha		Nafta	
Narrator		Narrador	
Nausea	Náusea		
Nautical		Náutico	
Nebula	Nébula		
Necessary		Necesario	
Nectar	Nectar		
Negro	Negro		
Negroid		Negroide	
Nemesis	Némesis		
Neocortex	Neocortex		
Neon	Neón		
Neoprene		Neopreno	
Neptune		Neptuno	

Charles Mazal-Cami

English	Spanish Same Spelling	Spanish Slightly Different Spelling	Notes
Nerve		Nervio	
Net (adj.)		Neto	
Neuroma	Neuroma		
Neutron	Neutrón		
Nevada	Nevada		
Nicaragua	Nicaragua		
Nickel		Niquel	
Nicotine		Nicotina	
Nitrogen		Nitrógeno	
Nodule		Nódulo	
Note		Anotar	(verb)
Note		Nota	(noun)
Notice		Noticia	
Nova	Nova		
Novel		Novela	
Nucleus		Núcleo	
Nylon	Nylon		
Nymph		Nimfa	
Oasis	Oásis		
Obedience		Obediencia	
Object		Objeto	
Obscene		Obsceno	
Observe		Observar	(verb)
Observatory		Observatorio	
Obsolete		Obsoleto	
Obstacle		Obstáculo	
Obtuse		Obtuso	
Occult		Oculto	
Occupant		Ocupante	
Occurence		Ocurrencia	
Ocean		Oceano	
Ochre		Ocre	
Octagon		Octágono	
Octane		Octano	
Octanol	Octanol		
Octave		Octavo	
Offence		Ofensa	
Offend		Ofender	(verb)
Office		Oficina	

English	Spanish Same Spelling	Spanish Slightly Different Spelling	Notes
Ogre		Ogro	
Ohm		Ohmio	
Oleander		Oleandro	
Olecranon	Olecranón		
Oleo	Oleo		
Oligarchy		Oligarquía	
Omega	Omega		
Omit		Omitir	(verb)
Omnibus	Omnibús		
Onyx		Ónix	
Opal		Ópalo	
Opaque		Opaco	
Opera	Ópera		
Opium		Opio	
Opportune		Oportuno	
Oratory		Oratorio	
Orbit		Órbita	
Orchestra		Orquesta	
Orchid		Orquidia	
Order [noun]		Orden	
Order [command]		Ordenar	(verb)
Ordinary		Ordinario	
Organ		Órgano	
Orgy		Orgía	
Orient		Orientar	(verb)
Origin		Origen	
Oriole		Oriol	
Ornate		Ornato	
Orthodox		Ortodoxo	
Osmium		Osmio	
Overture		Overtura	
Ovule		Óvulo	
Oxygen		Oxígeno	
Ozone		Ozona	
Pachiderm		Paquidermo	
Pagan		Pagano	
Pagoda	Pagoda		
Pajamas		Pijamas	
Pakistan	Pakistán		

Charles Mazal-Cami

English	Spanish Same Spelling	Spanish Slightly Different Spelling	Notes
Pakistani	Pakistani		
Palace		Palacio	
Palladium		Paladio	
Palm		Palma	
Panacea	Panacéa		
Panache	Panache		
Panama	Panamá		
Pancreas	Pancreas		
Panda	Panda		
Pandemonium		Pandemonio	
Panel	Pánel [group]	Panal	[for bees]
Panorama	Panorama		
Pantaloon [trousers]		Pantalón	
Pantheon		Panteón	
Panther		Pantera	
Pantomime		Pantomima	
Papaya	Papaya		
Papyrus		Papiro	
Paraffin		Parafina	
Paragon	Paragón		
Paraguay	Paraguay		
Parallel		Paralela	
Paralysis		Parálisis	
Paramo	Páramo		
Paranoia	Paranoia		
Parasite		Parásito	
Parasol	Parasol		
Parcel		Parcela	
Pardon		Perdón	
Pardon [forgive]		Perdonar	(verb)
Parenthesis		Paréntesis	
Paris	París		
Park [garden]		Parque	
Part		Parte	
Particle		Partícula	
Parquet	Parquet		
Pass		Pase	
Passage		Pasaje	
Passion		Pasión	

English	Spanish *Same Spelling*	Spanish *Slightly Different Spelling*	Notes
Passport		Pasaporte	
Pasta [food]	Pasta		
Paste		Pasta	(noun)
Paste		Empastar	(verb)
Pastel [color]	Pastel [also means "cake"]		
Pasture		Pastura	
Patience		Paciencia	
Patient		Paciente	
Patio	Patio		
Patriarch		Patriarca	
Patrimony		Patrimonio	
Patriot		Patriota	
Patron	Patrón		
Pavillion		Pabellón	
Pelican		Pelícano	
Pellagra		Pelagra	
Pelvis	Pelvis		
Penicillin		Penicilina	
Penitenciary		Penitenciaría	
Pentagon		Pentágono	
Penumbra	Penumbra		
Peon	Peón		
Per capita	Per cápita		
Percolator		Percolador	
Peregrine		Peregrino	
Perfect		Perfecto	
Perfume	Perfume		
Pergola	Pérgola		
Period		Periodo	
Peroxide		Peróxido	
Person		Persona	
Perpetual		Perpetuo	
Persona	Persona		
Perverse		Perverso	
Pervert		Perverto	
Peso	Peso		
Pesticide		Pesticida	
Pestilence		Pestilencia	
Petal		Pétalo	

Charles Mazal-Cami

English	Spanish Same Spelling	Spanish Slightly Different Spelling	Notes
Petroleum		Petroleo	
pH	pH		
Phallus		Falo	
Phantasm		Fantasma	
Pharmacy		Farmacia	
Phase		Fase	
Phenol		Fenol	
Philosophy		Filosofía	
Phoenix		Fénix	
Photo		Foto	
Photodetector		Fotodetector	
Photographer		Fotógrafo	
Photon		Fotón	
Phrase		Frase	
Physics		Física	
Piano	Piano		
Pica	Pica		
Picaro	Pícaro		
Piezo	Piezo		
Pilot		Piloto	(noun)
Pilot [the verb]		Pilotear	(verb)
Pimento		Pimiento	
Piña Colada	Piña Colada		
Piñata	Piñata		
Pine [tree]		Pino	
Pinion [nut]		Piñón	
Pint		Pinta	
Pioneer		Pionero	
Pipe		Pipa	
Pirate		Pirata	
Pirahna		Piraña	
Pistachio		Pistacho	
Pistol		Pistola	
Piston	Pistón		
Piton	Pitón		
Pivot		Pivote	
Pivot [the verb]		Pivotear	(verb)
Placebo	Placebo		
Placenta	Placenta		

English	Spanish Same Spelling	Spanish Slightly Different Spelling	Notes
Placid		Plácido	
Plan	Plan		(noun)
Plan		Planear	(verb)
Plane (flat)		Plano	
Plane (to glide)		Planear	(verb)
Planet		Planeta	
Planetoid		Planetóide	
Plant [factory or flora]		Planta	(noun)
Plaque		Placa	
Plasma	Plasma		
Platelet		Plateleta	
Platinum		Platino	
Plumage	Plumage		
Pneumonia		Neumonía	
Podium		Podio	
Poem		Poema	
Poet		Poeta	
Polaris	Polaris		
Pole (north)		Polo	
Police		Policía	
Politics		Política	
Politico	Político		
Polka	Polka		
Pollen		Polen	
Polo	Polo		
Polyp		Pólipo	
Pomade		Pomada	
Pontoon		Pontón	
Portafolio	Portafolio		
Portfolio		Portafolio	
Potassium		Potasio	
Potent		Potente	
Practice		Práctica	
Precede		Preceder	(verb)
Precedence		Precedencia	
Precious		Precioso	
Precise		Preciso	
Premier	Premier		
Prepare	Prepare		

English	Spanish Same Spelling	Spanish Slightly Different Spelling	Notes
Present		Presente	(adv.)
Preserve (as in Jam)		Preserva	(noun)
Preserve		Preservar	(verb)
Presidium		Presidio	
Presto	Presto		
Pretext		Pretexto	
Previous		Previo	
Prima donna		Primadona	
Primary		Primario	
Princess		Princesa	
Prism		Prisma	
Prison		Prisión	
Prisoner		Prisionero	
Privacy		Privacía	
Privilege		Privilegio	
Problem		Problema	
Process [method]		Proceso	(noun)
Process		Procesar	(verb)
Procurator		Procurador	
Profane		Profano	
Professor		Profesor	
Progress		Progreso	
Progress [go forward]		Progresar	(verb)
Prohibit		Prohibir	(verb)
Project		Proyecto	
Project [thrust]		Proyectar	(verb)
Prolapse		Prolapso	
Prologue		Prólogo	
Promise		Promesa	(noun)
Promise		Prometer	(verb)
Propaganda	Propaganda		
Propane		Propano	
Propellor		Propela	
Prophet		Profeta	
Prosaic		Prosaico	
Prose		Prosa	
Prospect		Prospecto	
Prostate		Próstata	
Prostitute		Prostituta	

English	Spanish Same Spelling	Spanish Slightly Different Spelling	Notes
Protagonist		Protagonista	
Proton	Protón		
Psychosis		Sicosis	
Pulse		Pulso	
Pupa	Pupa		
Pupil (eye)		Pupila	
Pure [100%]		Puro	
Puré [made paste]		Puré	
Purge		Purga	
Purge [vacate]		Purgar	(verb)
Purulent		Purulento	
Pus	Pús		
Putrid		Pútrido	
Pyramid		Pirámide	
Python		Pitón	
Quarantine		Cuarentena	
Quark	Qüark		
Quart		Cuarto	
Quartet		Cuarteto	
Quartz		Cuarzo	
Quarternary		Cuartenario	
Quasi	Quasi		
Quebec	Quebec		
Quest		Cuesta	
Question		Cuestión	
Quinella		Quiniela	
Quinine		Quinina	
Quintet		Quinteto	
Quintuple	Quíntuple		
Quito	Quito		
Quota		Cuota	
Rabbi		Rabino	
Rabies		Rabia	
Radiant		Radiante	
Radiator		Radiador	
Radio	Radio		
Radioisotope		Radioisótopo	
Radium		Radio	
Radius		Radio	

English	Spanish Same Spelling	Spanish Slightly Different Spelling	Notes
Radon	Radón		
Rally	Rally		
Ranch		Rancho	
Rancid		Ráncido	
Range		Rango	
Rapid		Rápido	
Rapt		Rapto	
Rare		Raro	
Rasp		Raspa	
Rat		Rata	
Rattan		Ratán	
Rayon	Rayón		
Realm		Realmo	
Reason		Razón	
Reason [the verb]		Razonar	(verb)
Rebel [the noun]		Rebelde	
Rebel [the verb]		Rebelar	(verb)
Rebellion		Rebelión	
Rebozo	Rebozo		
Recalcitrant		Recalcitrante	
Recess		Receso	
Reciprocal		Recíproco	
Recite		Recitar	(verb)
Recluse		Recluso	
Rectitude		Rectitud	
Rectum		Recto	
Reduce		Reducir	(verb)
Redundant		Redundante	
Reference		Referencia	
Reflex		Reflejo	
Reform		Reforma	
Refrigerator		Refrigerador	
Regal	Regal		
Regalia	Regalia		
Regent		Regente	
Regimen	Régimen		
Regiment		Regimiento	
Region	Región		
Register		Registro	

English	Spanish Same Spelling	Spanish Slightly Different Spelling	Notes
Regular	Regular		
Regulator		Regulador	
Relapse		Relapso	
Religion	Religión		
Remedy		Remedio	(noun)
Remedy		Remediar	(verb)
Remit		Remitir	(verb)
Remnant		Remanente	
Remote		Remoto	
Rent		Renta	
Repertoire		Repertorio	
Replete		Repleto	
Replica	Réplica		
Report [document]		Reporte	(noun)
Report [notify]		Reportar	(verb)
Represent		Representar	(verb)
Repressor		Represor	
Reproduce		Reproducir	(verb)
Reptile		Reptil	
Repugnance		Repugnancia	
Reserve [spare]		Reserva [noun]	
Reserve [keep apart]		Reservar [verb]	
Reservoir		Reservorio	
Reside		Residir	(verb)
Residence		Residencia	
Residue		Residuo	
Resilience		Resilencia	
Resilient		Resilente	
Resin		Resina	
Resist		Resistir	(verb)
Resolute		Resoluto	
Respect [reference to]		Respecto	
Respect		Respetar	(verb)
Respirator		Respirador	
Rest [what's left]		Resto	
Restaurant	Restaurant		
Resumé		Resumen	
Retard		Retardar	(verb)
Retort		Retorta	

Charles Mazal-Cami

English	Spanish Same Spelling	Spanish Slightly Different Spelling	Notes
Retrocede (to withdraw)		Retroceder	(verb)
Retrovirus	Retrovirus		
Return		Retorno	
Reunion	Reunión		
Reverend		Reverendo	
Reverse		Reversa	
Revolver	Revolver		
Rhapsody		Rapsodia	
Rhyme		Rima	
Ridicule		Ridiculizar	(verb)
Rifle	Rifle		
Rime		Rima	
Rite		Rito	
Rob		Robar	(verb)
Robot	Robot		
Robust		Robusto	
Romance	Romance		
Rose		Rosa	
Rosette		Roseta	
Roster	Róster		
Roulette		Ruleta	
Routine		Rutina	
Rubidium		Rubidio	
Rude		Rudo	
Ruin		Ruina	(noun)
Ruin [the verb]		Arruinar	(verb)
Rumba	Rumba		
Saccharine		Sacarina	
Salamander		Salamandra	
Salami	Salami		
Salary		Salario	
Salmon	Salmón		
Salmonella		Salmonela	
Salon	Salón		
Salvo	Salvo		
Samba	Samba		
Sandal		Sandalia	
Sane		Sano	
Sanguinary		Sanguinario	

English	Spanish Same Spelling	Spanish Slightly Different Spelling	Notes
Sanguine		Sanguineo	
Sarcasm		Sarcasmo	
Satelite	Satélite		
Satire		Sátiro	
Sauna	Sauna		
Sauté	Sauté		
Savor [flavor]		Sabor	
Savor [the verb]		Saborear	(verb)
Saxon		Sajón	
Saxophone		Saxofón	
Scale		Escala	
Scallop		Escalopa	
Scandal		Escándalo	
Scapular		Escapular	
Scene		Escena	
Scholar		Escolar	
Sclerosis		Esclerosis	
Scorpion		Escorpión	[also Alacrán]
Scuba	Scuba		
Sculptor		Escultor	
Sculpture		Escultura	
Secret		Secreto	
Sedan	Sedán		
Seduce		Seducir	(verb)
Seduces		Seduce	
Selenium		Selenio	
Semen	Semen		
Semester		Semestre	
Semi	Semi		
Semifluid		Semifluido	
Seminar		Seminario	
Semolina	Semolina		
Senator		Senador	
Señor	Señor		
Señora	Señora		
Señorita	Señorita		
Sentence (prison)		Sentencia	
Sentence [to pronounce]		Sentenciar	(verb)
Sentiment		Sentimiento	

Charles Mazal-Cami

English	Spanish Same Spelling	Spanish Slightly Different Spelling	Notes
Separator		Separador	
Septum	Séptum		
Sepulchre		Sepulcro	
Serape		Sarape	
Serenade		Serenata	(noun)
Serenade		Serenar	(verb)
Serene		Sereno	
Series		Serie	
Sermon	Sermón		
Serpentine		Serpentina	
Service		Servicio	
Servile		Servil	
Servo	Servo		
Severe		Severo	
Sex		Sexo	
Sextet		Sexteto	
Sextuple	Séxtuple		
Sierra	Sierra		
Siesta	Siesta		
Sign (as in Zodiac)		Signo	
Signal		Señal	
Silence		Silencio	
Silence [the verb]		Silenciar	(verb)
Silica	Sílica		
Silicon	Silicón		
Silicone		Silicón	
Silo	Silo		
Simple	Simple		
Sinusitis	Sinusitis		
Siphon		Sifón	
Siren		Sirena	
Site		Sitio	
Skeleton		Esqueleto	
Ski	Ski (also Esquí)		
Socialist		Socialista	
Society		Sociedad	
Soda	Soda		
Sodomy		Sodomía	
Solemn		Solemne	

English	Spanish Same Spelling	Spanish Slightly Different Spelling	Notes
Solenoid		Solenóide	
Solid		Sólido	
Solitaire		Solitario	
Solo	Solo		
Sonata	Sonata		
Sonde		Sonda	
Soprano	Soprano		
Sorbent		Sorbente	
Sorgo	Sorgo		
Soy		Soya	
Space		Espacio	
Spaghetti		Espagueti	
Spatula		Espátula	
Species		Especies	
Specimen		Especimen	
Spectrum		Espectro	
Speculum		Espéculo	
Sperm		Esperma	
Spermicide		Espermicida	
Sphere		Esfera	
Spirit		Espíritu	
Sponge		Esponja	
Spore		Espora	
Stalagmite		Estalagmita	
Stalagtite		Estalagtita	
Stamp (v.)		Estampar	(verb)
Standard		Estándar	
Stanza		Estanza	
Statue		Estatua	
Stature		Estatura	
Stellar		Estelar	
Stencil		Esténcil	
Stereo		Estereo	
Sterile		Estéril	
Stigma		Estigma	
Stress		Estresa	
Stupid		Estúpido	
Style		Estilo	
Suave	Suave		

Charles Mazal-Cami

English	Spanish Same Spelling	Spanish Slightly Different Spelling	Notes
Subaltern		Subalterno	
Sublime	Sublime		
Submarine		Submarino	
Subsist		Subsistir	(verb)
Suite	Suite		
Supernova	Supernova		
Support		Soporte	(noun)
Support		Soportar	(verb)
Syllable		Sílaba	
Symbol		Símbolo	
Synagogue		Sinagoga	
Syndicate		Sindicato	
Syndrome		Síndrome	
Synonym		Sinónimo	
Synopsis		Sinopsis	
Synthesis		Síntesis	
System		Sistema	
Swastika	Swástika		
Tobacco		Tabaco	
Tablet		Tableta	
Taboo		Tabú	
Taco	Taco		
Taffeta		Tafeta	
Talon	Talón		
Tamarind		Tamarindo	
Tambour		Tambor	
Tambourine		Tomborina	
Tampa	Tampa		
Tampon	Tampón		
Tanin		Tanina	
Tapioca	Tapioca		
Tarantula	Tarántula		
Tariff		Tarifa	
Taro	Taro		
Tarot	Tarot		
Tarpon	Tarpón		
Tartar		Tártaro	
Taurine		Taurino	
Tavern		Taverna	

English	Spanish Same Spelling	Spanish Slightly Different Spelling	Notes
Taverna	Taverna		
Taxi	Taxi		
Tea		Té	
Technic		Técnica	
Teflon	Teflón		
Telekinesis	Telekinesis		
Telephone		Teléfono	
Telex	Telex		
Tellurium		Telurio	
Temperature		Temperatura	
Temple		Templo	
Tempo	Tempo		
Tempura	Tempura		
Tendon	Tendón		
Tendril	Tendril		
Tennis		Tenis	
Tense		Tenso	
Tensile		Tensil	
Tequila	Tequila		
Termite		Termita	
Terrace		Terraza	
Terrapin		Terrapín	
Terrific		Terrífico	
Testimony		Testimonio	
Tetanus		Tétano	
Tetra	Tetra		
Tetracycline		Tetraciclina	
Texas	Texas		(also Tejas)
Texture		Textura	
Theory		Teoría	
Therapy		Terapia	
Thermonuclear		Termonuclear	
Thermos		Termo	
Thermostat		Termostato	
Thesaurus		Tesáuro	
Thesis		Tesis	
Tiger		Tigre	
Tint		Tinte	
Titan	Titán		

Charles Mazal-Cami

English	Spanish Same Spelling	Spanish Slightly Different Spelling	Notes
TNT	TNT		
Tobacco		Tabaco	
Toboggan		Tobogán	
Tomb		Tumba	
Toga	Toga		
Tombola	Tómbola		
Tombolo	Tómbolo		
Tone		Tono	
Torment		Tormenta	(noun)
Torment		Tormentar	(verb)
Torrid		Tórrido	
Torture		Tortura	(noun)
Torture		Torturar	(verb)
Topaz		Topacio	
Tornado	Tornado		
Torpedo	Torpedo		
Tostada	Tostada		
Tourist		Turista	
Toxin		Toxina	
Trachea		Traquea	
Trailer	Trailer		
Traitor		Traidor	
Trajectory		Trayectoria	
Tranquil		Tranquilo	
Transducer	Transducer		
Transform		Transformar	(verb)
Transformer		Transformador	
Transit		Tránsito	
Transit [to move]		Transitar	(verb)
Translucent		Translucente	
Translucid		Translúcido	
Transmit		Transmitir	(verb)
Transport		Transporte	(noun)
Transport		Transportar	(verb)
Trapezoid		Trapezoide	
Trauma	Trauma		
Triangle		Triángulo	
Tribe		Tríbu	
Tribute		Tributo	

English	Spanish Same Spelling	Spanish Slightly Different Spelling	Notes
Triceps	Triceps		
Trichina		Triquina	
Trichinosis		Triquinosis	
Tricot	Tricot		
Tricycle		Triciclo	
Trinity		Trinidad	
Triple	Triple		
Triumph		Triunfo	
Triumphal		Triunfal	
Triumphant		Triunfante	
Trombone		Trombón	
Trocar	Trócar		
Troop		Tropa	
Troy		Troya	
Tuba	Tuba		
Tube		Tubo	
Tulip		Tulipán	
Tumult		Tumulto	
Tuna	Tuna (also Atún)		
Tungsten		Tunsteno	
Tunica	Túnica		
Tunnel		Tunel	
Turban	Turbán		
Turbid		Túrbido	
Turbo	Turbo		
Type		Tipo	
Tyranny		Tiranía	
Tyrant		Tirano	
Ulcer		Ulcera	
Ulna	Ulna		
Ultimatum		Ultimato	
Ultra	Ultra		
Unguent		Ungüento	
Unicycle		Uniciclo	
Uniform		Uniforme	
Union	Unión		
Universe		Universo	
Uranium		Uranio	
Urban		Urbano	

English	Spanish Same Spelling	Spanish Slightly Different Spelling	Notes
Urea	Urea		
Urethra		Uretra	
Urine		Orina	
Urticaria	Urticaria		
Uruguay	Uruguay		
Use		Usar	(verb)
Utensil		Utensilio	
Vacant		Vacante	
Vagabond		Vagabundo	
Vagina	Vagina		
Valid		Válido	
Valley		Valle	
Vampire		Vampiro	
Vanilla		Vainilla	
Varnish		Barniz	
Vary		Varía	
Vast		Vasto	
Vehicle		Vehículo	
Velcro	Velcro		
Venezuela	Venezuela		
Vendetta		Vendeta	
Vent		Ventila	
Venture		Ventura	
Venturi	Venturí		
Venus	Venus		
Veranda	Veranda		
Verb		Verbo	
Verdict		Veredicto	
Verify		Verificar	(verb)
Vernier	Vernier		
Verse		Verso	
Vertebra	Vértebra		
Vertigo	Vértigo		
Vestibule		Vestíbula	
Veteran		Veterano	
Veto	Veto		
Viaduct		Viaducto	
Vibrant		Vibrante	
Vibrato	Vibrato		

English	Spanish Same Spelling	Spanish Slightly Different Spelling	Notes
Vibrator		Vibrador	
Vicar		Vicaro	
Victim		Víctima	
Victory		Victoria	
Vicuña	Vicuña		
Video	Video		
Videocassette	Videocassete		
Vigil		Vigilio	
Vigilance		Vigilancia	
Vigilante	Vigilante		
Vigoroso	Vigoroso		
Viking		Vikingo	
Villa	Villa		
Villain		Villano	
Vinyl		Vinilo	
Viola	Viola		
Violence		Violencia	
Violent		Violento	
Violet		Violeta	
Violin	Violín		
Virgin		Virgen	
Virile		Viril	
Virulence		Virulencia	
Virtuoso	Virtuoso		
Virus	Virus		
Visa	Visa		
Viscera	Víscera		
Viscous		Viscoso	
Visit		Visitar	(verb)
Visitant		Visitante	
Visiter		Visita	
Vista	Vista		
Vitamin		Vitamina	
Vitriform		Vitriforme	
Vitriol	Vitriol		
Vivace	Vivace		
Vivid		Vívido	
Vocable		Vocablo	
Vodka	Vodka		

Charles Mazal-Cami

English	Spanish	Spanish	Notes
	Same Spelling	Slightly Different Spelling	
Vogue		Voga	
Volatile		Volatil	
Volcano		Volcán	
Volt		Voltio	
Volume		Volumen	
Voluntary		Voluntario	
Volunteer [noun]		Voluntario	
Vomit [noun]		Vómito	
Vomit [verb]		Vomitar	(verb)
Voodoo		Vudú	
Vortex	Vórtex		
Vote [noun]		Voto	
Vote [verb]		Votar	(verb)
Wagon		Vagón	
Waltz		Vals	
Watt	Watt [also Vatio]		
Xenon	Xenón		
Yoga	Yoga		
Yoghurt	Yoghurt [also Yogurt]		
Yucatan	Yucatán		
Yucca	Yucca [also Yuca]		
Zebra	Zebra [also Cebra]		
Zebu		Cebú	
Zero		Cero	
Zinc	Zinc		
Zircon	Zircón		
Zodiac		Zodiaco	
Zone		Zona	
Zoom	Zoom		(also Zúm)

Interesting, yes?

**Remember, these were all in *addition* to those words
that you have *already* learned with the Rules!**

"Matching Words" : *What the censor left out.*

The foregoing word list was the result of a cursory search through a common dictionary and by no means represents all of the fascinatingly similar English-Spanish words. In addition to those listed, there are hundreds more that, although close, were not close enough to meet the criteria of the list (e.g., *Eng.* Pavement - *Sp.* Pavimento). Additionally, there are hundreds of medical, technical and scientific terms that were omitted as well as those that, in English, have fallen out of common usage, although they continue to be listed in the dictionary.   For example, have you ever wondered why the candy dispenser ar the corner grocer is called a vending machine? *Vending* machine? Why not *selling* machine? Well, many people may not realize it but to *vend*, in English, is to *sell!*   Curiously, *vender* in Spanish, is...you guessed it: *to sell!*

Appendix

COLORS, TEXTURES & SHAPES

The Colors:

blue	**azul**	red	**rojo**
green	**verde**	yellow	**amarillo**
white	**blanco**	black	**negro**
orange	**anaranjado**	purple	**morado**
pink	**rosa**	gray	**grís**
brown	**café**	sepia	**sepia**
violet	**violeta**	magenta	**magenta**
blue-green	**azul verdoso**	ivory	**marfil**

and Shades:

light	**claro**	dark	**oscuro**
pastel	**pastel**	deep	**profundo**

Textures:
for Feminine-gendered nouns, the adjectives that end in "...o", will end in "...a"
(See Chapter 17)

smooth	**liso**	rough	**rugoso**
slippery (or slick)	**resbaloso**	sharp	**filoso**
pointed	**picudo**	soft	**suave**
hard	**duro**	wet	**mojado**
dry	**seco**	clean	**limpio**
dirty	**sucio**	sticky	**pegajoso**
granular	**granoso**	spongey	**esponjoso**
hot	**caliente**	cold	**frio**
frozen	**congelado**	warm	**tibio**

The Shapes:

for Feminine-gendered nouns, the adjectives that end in "...o", will end in "...a"
(See Chapter 17)

square	**cuadrado**	round	**redondo**
cube	**cubo**	rectangular	**rectangular**
oval	**ovalado**	plane	**plano**
cylindrical	**cilíndrico**	sphere	**esfera**
long	**largo**	short	**corto**
tall	**alto**	thin	**delgado**
fat	**gordo**	thick (or stout)	**grueso**
skinny	**flaco**	obese	**obeso**
large	**grande**	small	**pequeño**
tiny	**pequeñísimo**	enormous	**enorme**

Parts of the Body

head	**cabeza**	cheek	**mejilla**
face	**cara**	eyes	**ojos**
nose	**nariz**	ears	**oídos**
mouth	**boca**	teeth	**dientes**
tongue	**lengua**	forehead	**frente**
hair	**cabello** [or pelo]	beard	**barba**
chin	**mentón**	eye-lid	**párpado**
neck	**cuello**	shoulders	**hombros**
arm	**brazo**	wrist	**muñeca**
hand	**mano**	fingers	**dedos**
fingernails	**uñas**	stomach [area]	**vientre**
back	**espalda**	hips	**caderas**
spine	**espina**	upper leg	**muslo**
knee	**rodilla**	ankle	**tobillo**
shin	**espinilla**	foot	**pié**
heel	**talón**	toe	**dedo del pié**

Appendix
Useful Phrases

Taxi
Could you please call a Taxi for me?
> **Me puede llamar un Taxi, por favor?**

What is the fare to the (airport) (____ Hotel)?
> **Cuanto cuesta al (aereopuerto)(Hotel ___)?**

Please have a Taxi here at ____ o'clock.
> **Por favor tenga un Taxi aquí a las ___ horas.**

Airport/car-rental
Which way is the airport?
> **Hacia adonde está el Aereopuerto?**

Where is the rental-car booth?
> **Adonde está la oficina de auto-renta?**

Do you have any cars available?
> **Tiene autos disponibles?**

Where is the ____ airlines ticket-counter?
> **Adonde está el mostrador de _____?**

Where do I pick up my luggage?
> **En donde recojo mi equipaje?**

I have a total of ____bags.
> **Tengo un total de ___ maletas.**

I'm travelling on flight number ___.
> **Viajo en el vuelo número ____.**

Hotel
I'm staying at the ____ hotel.
> **Estoy hospedado en el hotel ____.**

Do you have any rooms available?
> **Tiene cuartos disponibles?**

What are your room rates?
> **Cuanto es la tarifa?**

Do you have a weekly rate?
> **Tiene una tarifa semanal?**

I need a single room.
> **Necesito un cuarto sencillo.**

I need a double room.
> **Necesito un cuarto doble.**

I prefer a queen-size bed.
> **Prefiero una cama "queen-size".**

I need two single beds.
> **Necesito dos camas sencillas.**

Useful Phrases (cont.)

I need an extra cot.

Necesito un catre adicional.

I need a baby bed.

Necesito una cuna.

Which is way is the restaurant?

Adonde está el restorán?

Could you please bring some extra towels?

Podria traer unas toallas adicionales, por favor?

Could you bring me an additional pillow, please?

Podria traerme una almohada adicional, por favor?

Please bring me some bottled water.

Me trae agua embotellada, por favor.

Do you have an ice machine?

Tienen una máquina de hielo?

Where is the ice machine?

Adonde está la máquina de hielo?

Is there laundry service available?

Hay servicio de lavanderia?

Is there dry-cleaning available?

Hay servicio de tintoreria?

I need my clothes by (tomorrow) (today).

Necesito mi ropa para (mañana) (hoy).

What time is check-out?

Cual es la hora de salida?

Could you send a bell-boy to my room?

Podria mandar un botones a mi cuarto?

Please take my luggage to the lobby.

Lléve mis maletas al lobby, por favor.

Restaurant

Could you please bring a menu?

Podria traerme un menú, por favor?

Do you have a menu in English?

Tiene un menú en Inglés?

What is your specialty?

Cual es la especialidad de la casa?

What is your daily dish today?

Cual es el platillo del dia?

I would like to order (a cocktail) **Quiero ordenar (un coctel)**

(a salad)   **(una ensalada)**

(a dessert)   **(un postre)**

Please bring me some water.

Me trae agua, por favor.

Please bring me a napkin.

Me trae una servilleta, por favor.

Please bring me a (fork) (spoon) (knife).

Me trae (un tenedor) (una cuchara)
(un cuchillo), por favor.

Could I see your dessert tray, please?

Podria ver los postres, por favor?

Could I have the check, please?

Me trae la cuenta, por favor?

<u>NOTE</u>: **There are separate words in Spanish to differentiate between HOT (Caloric) and <u>*HOT*</u> (Spicey).**

HOT (Caloric) in Spanish is **CALIENTE.**

HOT (Spicey) in Spanish is **PICANTE.**

Hot *SAUCE* (Spicey) is **Salsa *picante.***

Hot *SOUP* (Caloric) is **Sopa *caliente.***

<u>Tips</u>

In a Restaurant, a tip is generally 15% of the bill. In Mexico, there is a Value-Added Tax (I.V.A.) of 15% which will usually appear on your bill. Your tip should be roughly equivalent to that Tax (not 15% of the total Meal + Tax!). If it is a small bill (coffee, softdrinks, etc.), figure on 20-25% of the bill as a tip.

Throughout Latinamerica, tips for carrying luggage (such as bellboys in hotels) is generally equivalent (roughly) to fifty cents (U.S.) for each piece of luggage if there are three or more. Minimum tip would be regarded as the local equivalent of $1.25, U.S.

Appendix

Useful Words

INSECTS & ANIMALS	INSECTOS Y ANIMALES	EDIBLES	COMESTIBLES
Ant	Hormiga	Apple	Manzana
Antelope	Antílope	Artichoke	Alcachofa
Armadillo	Armadillo	Bacon	Tocino
Bee	Abeja (or Colmena)	Butter	Mantequilla
Bird	Pájaro	Cabbage	Col
Buffalo	Búfalo	Candy	Dulce
Bull	Toro	Carrot	Zanahoria
Butterfly	Mariposa	Cauliflower	Coliflor
Cat	Gato	Chicken	Pollo
Chicken	Gallina [f]	Chocolate	Chocolate
Cockroach	Cucaracha	Coffee	Café
Cow	Vaca	Corn (on the cob)	Elote
Deer	Venado	Cucumber	Pepino
Dog	Perro	Dessert	Postre
Dolphin	Delfín	Egg	Huevo
Donkey	Burro	Fish	Pescado
Elephant	Elefante	Garlic	Ajo
Flea	Pulga	Ham	Jamón
Fly	Mosca	Hamburger	Hamburguesa
Goat	Cabra	Lemon	Limón (see Note)
Horse	Caballo	Lettuce	Lechuga
Hog	Puerco	Lime	Limón or Lima (seeNote)
Giraffe	Jirafa	Meat	Carne
Gnat	Jején	Melon	Melón
Kangaroo	Kangúro	Milk	Leche
Lamb	Borrego (or Carnero)	Onion	Cebolla
Leopard	Leopardo	Oregano	Orégano
Lion	León	Parsley	Perejil
Monkey	Mono (or Chango)	Pepper (spice)	Pimienta
Mosquitoe	Mosquito (or Mosco)	Pork	Puerco
Mouse	Ratón	Potatoe	Papa
Parrot	Perico	Radish	Rábano
Pig	Puerco	Ribs	Costillas
Rabbit	Conejo	Rice	Arroz
Rat	Rata	Salt	Sal
Rooster	Gallo	Sauce	Salsa
Scorpion	Alacrán (or Escorpión)	Shrimp	Camarón
Snake	Serpiente (or Víbora)	Sirloin	Sirloin
Spider	Araña	Soup	Sopa
Tiger	Tigre	Spaghetti	Espagetti
Whale	Ballena	Steak	Filete
Worm	Lombriz	Sugar	Azucar
Zebra	Cebra	T-Bone	Tibón
		Tomatoe	Jitomate
		Yoghurt	Yoghurt

NOTE: In English, a <u>Lemon</u> is a yellow citric fruit and a <u>Lime</u> is a smaller, green citric fruit. In Spanish, both of these are known by the same name: **Limón.** A third fruit which is about the size of an orange, is semi-sweet with an almost transparent pulp, is known in Spanish as a **LIMA.** The "Lima" is almost unkown in North America and Europe, although it is common in Central & South America. English-speaking people often make the mistake of asking for "Lima" when, what they want, is "Limón".

Charles Mazal-Cami

CLOTHES	ROPA	TOILETRIES	ARTICULOS DE BAÑO
Bath Robe	Bata de baño	After-shave lotion	Loción para afeitar
Belt	Cinturón	Cold Cream	Crema teatrical
Blouse	Blusa	Comb	Peine
Button	Botón	Conditioner	Acondicionador
Boots	Botas	Clothes brush	Cepillo para ropa
Brassiere	Brasier	Fingernail polish	Esmalte de uñas
Cap	Cachucha	Hand cream	Crema de manos
Coat	Saco	Hair dryer	Secador de pel
Contact lenses	Lentes de contacto	Hair-removal wax	Cera depilante
Eyeglasses	Lentes	Hair pin	Horquilla para cabello
Hat	Sombrero	Nail clippers	Corta-uñas
Handkerchief	Pañuelo	Perfume	Perfume
Jacket	Chamarra	Toilet paper	Papel de baño
Overcoat	Abrigo	Towel	Toalla
Panties	Pantaletas	Sanitary Napkins	Toallas sanitarias
Pants	Pantalón	(also by brand name: Kotex, Tampax, etc.)	
Robe	Bata	Hand towel	Toalla de mano
Scarf	Bufanda	Alcohol	Alcohol
Skirt	Falda	Shaving cream	Crema para afeitar
Shirt	Camisa	Soap	Jabón
Shoe laces	Agujetas	Polish remover	Removedor de esmalte
Shoes	Zapatos	Razor handle	Rastrillo para afeitar
Stockings	Medias	Razor blade	Hoja para afeitar
Slippers	Pantuflas	Shampoo	Shampú
Socks	Calcetines		
Sweater	Suéter		
T-shirt	Camiseta	LEISURE TIME	DESCANSO
Underwear (men's)	Calzones	Movie	Cine
Undershirt (men's)	Camiseta	Nightclub	Club Nocturno
Vest	Chaleco	Jai-Alai	Frontón
Wig	Peluca	Bullfight	Corrida de Toros
		Race Track	Hipódromo
		Discoteque	Discoteca
SHOPS	TIENDAS	Cock fight	Pelea de gallos
Supermarket	Supermercado	Tours	Recorridos
Department Store	Almacén	Restaurant	Restaurant
Hardware	Tlapaleria	Golf club	Club de Golf
Shoe store	Zapateria	Beach	Playa
Grocery store	Abarrotería	Fishing boat	Barco de pesca
Leather goods	Peleteria	Excursion	Excursión
Pharmacy	Farmacia	Fair	Feria
Arts & crafts	Artesanias	Circus	Circo
Jewelry store	Joyeria	Park	Parque
Sporting goods	Deportes	Zoo	Zoológico
Boutique	Boutique	Bar	Bar (or Cantina]
Art Gallery	Galeria de arte	Museum	Muséo
Beauty salón	Salón de belleza	Boxing arena	Arena de boxéo
Barbershop	Peluquería	Dance hall	Salón de baile
Bakery	Panaderia	Water skiing	Esquí aquático
Antiques	Antigüedades	Video rent	Renta de vidéos
Flower shop	Florería	Cabaret	Cabaret

SERVICES	SERVICIOS	TRAVELER	VIAJERO
Airlines	Aereolíneas	Alarm Clock	Despertador
Airport	Aereopuerto	Bathtub	Tina
Apartments	Apartamentos	Blouse	Blusa
Architect	Arquitecto	Book	Libro
Bar	Bar (or Cantina)	Brassiere	Brasier
Barbershop	Peluquería	Chair	Silla
Book Store	Librería	Comb	Peine
Bus	Autobús (or Camión)	Curtain	Cortina
Candy Store	Dulcería	Door	Puerta
Chofer (Driver)	Chofer	Dress	Vestido
Cleaners	Tintorería	Elevator	Elevador
Clothing Store	Almacén de Ropa	Emergency Exit	Salidade Emergencia
Cook	Cocinera (f) or Cocinero (m)	Gratuity (TIP)	Propina
Department Store	Almacenes	Hairbrush	Cepillo para cabello
Dentist	Dentista	Hand cream	Crema de manos
Doctor	Doctor	Ice	Hielo
Drugstore	Farmacia	Jacket	Chamarra
Florist	Florería	Jewelry	Joyería
Gardener	Jardinero	Key	Llave
Gas Station	Gasolinería	Lock	Candado
Golf course	Campo de Golf	Magazine	Revista
Gynecologist	Ginecólogo	Menu	Menú (also Carta)
Hairdresser	Salón de Belleza	Money	Dinero
Hardware store	Ferretería (also Tlapalería)	Nail polish	Esmalte para uñas
Hotel	Hotel	Newspaper	Periódico
Jewelry store	Joyería	Overcoat	Abrigo
Laundromat	Lavandería	Panties	Pantaletas
Lawyer	Abogado	Purse	Bolsa de mano
Maid	Recamarera	Razor	Hoja de afeitar
Manager	Gerente	Refrigerator	Refrigerador
Market	Mercado	Room	Cuarto
Mechanic	Mecánico	Shampoo	Shampú
Motel	Motel	Shaving lather	Crema de afeitar
Movers	Mudanza	Shirt	Camisa
Oculist (eye Dr.)	Oculista	Shoes	Zapatos
Office	Oficina	Shoe polish	Grasa para zapatos
Optical supply	Optica	Shoestrings	Agujetas
Optometrist	Optometrista	Shower	Regadera
Pediatrician	Pediatra	Soap	Jabón
Photographer	Fotógrafo	Socks	Calcetines
Pier (marine)	Muelle	Stairs	Escaleras
Police Department	Delegación	Stockings	Medias
Policeman	Policía	Table	Mesa
Restaurant	Restaurant	Telephone directory	Directorio telefónico
Shoe store	Zapatería	Toothbrush	Cepillo de dientes
Supermarket	Supermercado	Toothpaste	Pasta dentífrica
Swimming pool	Alberca	Trousers	Pantalones
Tabacconist	Tabaquería	Umbrella	Paraguas
Taxi	Táxi	Underwear	Ropa interior
Tennis court	Cancha de ténis	Wallet	Cartera
Travel Agency	Agencia de Viajes	Water (bottled)	Agua (embotellada)
Waiter	Mesero (m) or Mesera (f)	Window	Ventana

OFFICE	OFICINA	KITCHEN	COCINA
Ballpoint Pen	Bolígrafo	Can opener	Abrelatas
Calculator	Calculadora	Coffee maker	Cafetera
Cash register	Caja registradora	Dish	Plato
Computer	Computadora	Dishwasher	Lavadora de platos
Copying Machine	Copiadora	Fork	Tenedor
Counter	Mostrador	Freezer	Congeladora
Desk	Escritorio	Knife	Cuchillo
Eraser	Borrador	Microwave oven	Horno de Microónda
Fax Machine	Fax	Mixer (cake)	Batidora
Folders	Carpetas	Oven	Horno
Ink	Tinta	Pan	Sartén
Paper	Papel	Pantry	Alacena
Paper clip	Grapa (or Clip)	Pot	Olla
Pen	Pluma	Refrigerator	Refrigerador
Pencil	Lápiz	Serving dish	Platón
Recorder	Grabadora	Sink	Fregadero
Rubber band	Liga	Stir spoon	Cucharón
Stapler	Engrapadora	Stove	Estufa
Telephone	Teléfono	Spatula	Espátula
Telex	Telex	Towel (dish)	Trapo de cocina
Typewriter	Máquina de escribir		

DAYS OF THE WEEK

		MONTH	MES
Monday	**Lunes**	January	**Enero**
Tuesday	**Martes**	February	**Febrero**
Wednesday	**Miércoles**	March	**Marzo**
Thursday	**Jueves**	April	**Abril**
Friday	**Viernes**	May	**Mayo**
Saturday	**Sábado**	June	**Junio**
Sunday	**Domingo**	July	**Julio**
		August	**Agosto**
		September	**Septiembre**

FURNITURE   MUEBLES

		October	**Octubre**
Table	Mesa	November	**Noviembre**
Chair	Silla	December	**Diciembre**
Bed	Cama		
Baby bed	Cuna		
Armoir	Armario		
Couch	Sillón		
Desk	Escritorio		
Garden furniture	Muebles de Jardín		
Bar stool	Silla de barra		
Wheel chair	Silla de ruedas		

Numbers

Números

ONE	....	**UNO**
TWO	....	**DOS**
THREE	....	**TRES**
FOUR	....	**CUATRO**
IVE	....	**CINCO**
SIX	....	**SEIS**
SEVEN	....	**SIETE**
EIGHT	....	**OCHO**
NINE	....	**NUEVE**
TEN	....	**DIEZ**
ELEVEN	....	**ONCE**
TWELVE	....	**DOCE**
THIRTEEN	....	**TRECE**
FOURTEEN	....	**CATORCE**
FIFTEEN	....	**QUINCE**
SIXTEEN	....	**DIECISEIS**
SEVENTEEN	....	**DIECISIETE**
EIGHTEEN	....	**DIECIOCHO**
NINETEEN	....	**DIECINUEVE**
TWENTY	....	**VEINTE**
TWENTY-ONE	....	**VEINTIUNO**
TWENTY-TWO	....	**VEINTIDOS** (ETC)
THIRTY	....	**TREINTA**
THIRTY-ONE	....	**TREINTA Y UNO**
THIRTY-TWO	....	**TREINTA Y DOS** (ETC)
FORTY	....	**CUARENTA**
FORTY-ONE	....	**CUARENTA Y UNO**
FORTY-TWO	....	**CUARENTA Y DOS** (ETC.)
FIFTY	....	**CINCUENTA**
FIFTY-ONE	....	**CINCUENTA Y UNO**
FIFTY-TWO	....	**CINCUENTA Y DOS** (ETC.)
SIXTY	....	**SESENTA**
SIXTY-ONE	....	**SESENTA Y UNO**
SIXTY-TWO	....	**SESENTA Y DOS** (ETC.)
SEVENTY	....	**SETENTA**
SEVENTY-ONE	....	**SETENTA Y UNO**
SEVENTY-TWO	....	**SETENTA Y DOS** (ETC.)
EIGHTY	....	**OCHENTA**
EIGHTY-ONE	....	**OCHENTA Y UNO**
EIGHTY-TWO	....	**OCHENTA Y DOS** (ETC.)
NINETY	....	**NOVENTA**
NINETY-ONE	....	**NOVENTA Y UNO**

Charles Mazal-Cami

NINETY-TWO	....	**NOVENTA Y DOS** (ETC.)
ONE HUNDRED	....	**CIEN**
ONE HUNDRED ONE	....	**CIENTO UNO**
ONE HUNDRED TEN	....	**CIENTO DIEZ**
ONE HUNDRED TWENTY	....	**CIENTO VEINTE** (ETC.)
TWO HUNDRED	....	**DOSCIENTOS**
TWO HUNDRED ONE	....	**DOSCIENTOS UNO**
TWO HUNDRED TEN	....	**DOSCIENTOS VEINTE** (ETC..)
THREE HUNDRED	....	**TRESCIENTOS**
FOUR HUNDRED	....	**CUATROCIENTOS**
FIVE HUNDRED	....	**QUINIENTOS**
SIX HUNDRED	....	**SEISCIENTOS**
SEVEN HUNDRED	....	**SETECIENTOS**
EIGHT HUNDRED	....	**OCHOCIENTOS**
NINE HUNDRED	....	**NOVECIENTOS**
ONE THOUSAND	....	**MIL**
ONE THOUSAND ONE HUNDRED	....	**MIL CIEN**
ONE THOUSAND ONE HUNDRED ONE...		**MIL CIENTO UNO**
TWO THOUSAND	....	**DOS MIL**
THREE THOUSAND	....	**TRES MIL**
FIVE THOUSAND	....	**CINCO MIL**
TEN THOUSAND	....	**DIEZ MIL** (ETC.)
ONE HUNDRED THOUSAND	....	**CIEN MIL**
FIVE HUNDRED THOUSAND	....	**QUINIENTOS MIL**
ONE MILLION	....	**UN MILLON**
TEN MILLION	....	**DIEZ MILLONES** (ETC.)
FIFTY MILLION	....	**CINCUENTA MILLONES**
ONE HUNDRED MILLION	....	**CIEN MILLONES**

USEFUL VERBS

Although we have learned many, many words in the preceding Chapters, including hundreds of verbs, there are thousands more in the Spanish language. Here are some additional Spanish verbs that have not been covered by the Rules and which you might find useful. You have already learned how to Conjugate these verbs in Chapter Eighteen.

**Remember that there are only three verb ENDINGS in Spanish:
....AR, ...ER and ....IR.**

The "silent subjects" appear in brackets:

Querer	(to Want)
[Yo] quiero	I want
[Tu] quieres	You want
[El] quiere	He wants
[Ella] quiere	She wants
[Usted] quiere [polite, sing.]	You want
[Ellos] quieren	They want
[Ellas] quieren	They want [f]
[Ustedes] quieren	You want [plural]
[Nosotros] queremos	We want

Necesitar	(to Need)
[Yo] necesito	I need
[Tu] necesitas	You need
[El] necesita	He needs
[Ella] necesita	She needs
[Usted] necesita [Polite, sing.]	You need
[Ellos] necesitan	They need
[Ellas] necesitan	They need [f]
[Ustedes] necesitan	You need [plural]
[Nosotros] necesitamos	We need

Sentir   (to Feel)

[Yo] siento   **I feel**
[Tu] sientes   **You feel**
[El] siente   **He feels**
[Ella] siente   **She feels**
[Usted] siente [Polite, sing.]   **You feel**
[Ellos] sienten   **They feel**
[Ellas] sienten   **They feel** [f]
[Ustedes] sienten   **You feel** [plural]
[Nosotros] sentimos   **We feel**

Hacer   (to Do or Make)

[Yo] hago   **I do/make**
[Tú] haces   **You do/make**
[El] hace   **He does/makes**
[Ella] hace   **She does/makes**
[Usted] hace [Polite, sing.]   **You do/make**
[Ellos] hacen   **They do/make**
[Ellas] hacen   **They do/make** [f]
[Ustedes] hacen   **You do/make** [plural]
[Nosotros] hacemos   **We do/make**

Ir   (to Go)

[Yo] voy   **I go**
[Tú] vas   **You go**
[El] va   **He goes**
[Ella] va   **She goes**
[Usted] va [Polite, sing.]   **You go**
[Ellos] van   **They go**
[Ellas] van   **They go** [f]
[Ustedes] van   **You go** [plural]
[Nosotros] vamos   **We go**

Venir   (to Come)

[Yo] vengo   I come
[Tú] vienes   You come
[El] viene   He comes
[Ella] viene   She comes
[Usted] viene [Polite sing.]   You come
[Ellos] vienen   They come
[Ellas] vienen   They come [f]
[Ustedes] vienen   You come [plural]
[Nosotros] venimos   We come

Ver   (to See)

[Yo] veo   I see
[Tu] ves   You see
[El] ve   He sees
[Ella] ve   She sees
[Usted] ve [Polite, sing.]   You see
[Ellos] ven   They see
[Ellas] ven   They see [f]
[Ustedes] ven   You see [plural]
[Nosotros] vemos   We see

Comer   (to Eat)

[Yo] como   I eat
[Tú] comes   You eat
[El] come   He eats
[Ella] come   She eats
[Usted] come [Polite, sing.]   You eat
[Ellos] comen   They eat
[Ellas] comen   They eat [f]
[Ustedes] comen   You eat [plural]
[Nosotros] comemos   We eat

Deber	Must, Ought to, to Owe
[Yo] debo	I must/ought to/ owe
[Tú] debes	You must/ought to/ owe
[El] debe	He must/ought to/owes
[Ella] debe	She must/ought to/owes
[Usted] debe [Polite, sing.]	You must/ought to/owes
[Ellos] deben	They must/ought to/owe
[Ellas] deben	They must/ought to/owe [f]
[Ustedes] deben [Plural]	You must/ought to/owe[plur]
[Nosotros] debemos	We must/ought to/owe

Pagar	(to Pay)
[Yo] pago	I pay
[Tú] pagas	You pay
[El] paga	He pays
[Ella] paga	She pays
[Usted] paga [Polite, sing.]	You pay
[Ellos] pagan	They pay
[Ellas] pagan	They pay [f]
[Ustedes] pagan	You pay [plural]
[Nosotros] pagamos	We pay

Llevar	to Carry[away]; to Take [away] *also* to Wear
[Yo] llevo	I carry/take [away]
[Tú] llevas	You carry/take [away]
[El] lleva	He carries/takes [away]
[Ella] lleva	She carries/takes [away]
[Usted] lleva [Polite, sing.]	You carry/take [away]
[Ellos] llevan	They carry/take [away]
[Ellas] llevan	They carry/take [away] [f]
[Ustedes] llevan	You carry/take [away] [pl]
[Nosotros] llevamos	We carry/take [away]

Traer	(to Bring)
[Yo] traigo	I bring
[Tú] traes	You bring
[El] trae	He brings
[Ella] trae	She brings
[Usted] traiga [Polite, sing.]	You bring
[Ellos] traen	They bring
[Ellas] traen	They bring [f]
[Ustedes] traen	You bring [plural]
[Nosotros] traemos	We bring

Llamar	(to Call, to Name)
[Yo] llamo	I call
[Tú] llamas	You call
[El] llama	He calls
[Ella] llama	She calls
[Usted] llama [Polite, sing.]	You call
[Ellos] llaman	They call
[Ellas] llaman	They call [f]
[Ustedes] llaman	You call [plural]
[Nosotros] llamamos	We call

Poder	Can (do)
[Yo] puedo	I can
[Tu] puedes	You can
[El] puede	He can
[Ella] puede	She can
[Usted] puede [Polite, sing.]	You can
[Ellos] pueden	They can
[Ellas] pueden	They can [f]
[Ustedes] pueden	You can [plural]
[Nosotros] podemos	We can

CHEAT SHEET

The Major Rules

English	*Spanish*	*See page*
....tion	....ción	11
....ate	....ar	15
....ize	....izar	19
....al	....al	21
....ic	....ico	31
....ity	....idad	35
....ism (or ....ysm)	....ismo	39
....sion	....sión	43
....ous	....oso	45
....ent	....ente	49
....ally	....mente	53
....ary/ory	....ario/orio	57
....ble	....ble	61
....ive	....ivo	65

CHEAT SHEET

The Minor Rules

English	*Spanish*	*See page*
....ar	....ar	86
....ator	....ador	86
....cle	....culo	87
....copy	....copia	88
....ctor	....ctor	88
....ence	....encia	89
....ene	....eno	89
....graph	....grafo	89
....graphy	....grafía	90
....ical	....ico	90
....ify	....ificar	90
....ine	....ina	91
....ist	....ista	91
....ium	....io	92
....logy	....logía	93
....meter	....metro	93
....metry	....metría	94
....omy	....omía	94
....or (not <u>A</u>TOR or <u>CT</u>OR)	....or	94
....osis	....ósis	95
....plasma	....plasma	96
....scope	....scopio	96
....sty	....stía	96
....ume	....umir	97
....ure	....ura	97
....ute	....uto	98

About the Author

Charles Mazal-Cami was born in Mexico City, where he grew up and attended school in bilingual classrooms. Most of his childhood friends were also fluently bilingual, speaking both English and Spanish, and Charles recalls the special language they spoke among themselves, something he dubbed "Spanglish".

Charles dropped out of college and at nineteen was already in business for himself importing and selling medical equipment. He had rough times but his tenacity and entrepeneurial spirit eventually prevailed and he went on to establish many different and successful businesses throughout his life. He became involved in nearly every conceivable venture, from commercial fishing to the manufacture of plywood, computers and even orthopedic implants. Charles is an inventor and has the inventor's attitude that "there *must* be a better way" and over his lifetime has accummulated more than thirty patents. Many of his inventions have been in the biomedical field and he has contributed much to medical science. His inventions are used daily around the world and millions of people have benefited from his creativity.

Living in Mexico and being multilingual, Charles often found himself in the role of interpreter for friends and business associates, many of whom spoke only English. Although he tried to encourage them to learn another language, the reply was always the same: "it takes too much *time* and it's so *difficult!*" Charles finally decided to do something about it and set about to find a *better way*, launching himself into yet another career: writing.

This book is the result of Mazal-Cami's inventiveness, a totally fresh and *different* concept for learning a language. It reflects his boredom with conventional methods that teach the drudgery of grammar *before* getting into the essence of the language: the words. "Language is about *words*", he concluded, "not about rules and slots." As with so many other things, from heart-valves to insect traps and from catheters to pumps, this book will likely change the way that the Spanish language is taught.

As of this writing, Charles' first novel, *"An Eye for a Tooth"*, a terrorist thriller, is about to roll on the presses, disclosing yet another facet of his creative personality.

Here is what other publishers have said about this book!

PRENTICE HALL
"...an excellent contribution to the foreign language field"

TEACHERS COLLEGE PRESS
"...we feel there is a great deal of merit in your work"

WHITE CLIFFS MEDIA COMPANY
"...you have a terrific idea"

HOLLOWBROOK PUBLISHING
"We commend you for the work you have done on this subject."

SIMON & SCHUSTER
[the book] "...is such a nifty idea"

NATIONAL TEXTBOOK COMPANY
"...seems like an interesting concept"

J. WESTON WALCH, PUBLISHER
"We feel the concept is succinct and easy to read and use"

WALL & EMERSON
"...your book...is a neat idea."

KNACK PUBLISHING
"...can't believe it wasn't thought of before!"

PRAKKEN PUBLICATIONS
"...this does appear to be a concise and pointed approach"

Use this handy form to order additional copies of
"20,000 Words in Spanish, *in 20 Minutes!"*
<u>directly from the Publisher</u>!
(see reverse)

WOULD YOU
LIKE ANOTHER COPY
OF THIS BOOK?

Get a friend involved in learning Spanish!

Books make great (and memorable) gifts!

Just fill out the Order Blank below, enclose your check for $14.95 (+ $1.75 for *prompt* S&H) and mail it to:

Palabra Press
13423 Blanco Road, Suite 232
San Antonio, TX 78216

- ✂

Palabra Press
13423 Blanco Road, Suite 232
San Antonio, TX 78216

Please send me ____copies of
"20,000 Words in Spanish, *in 20 Minutes!*" (2nd Edition)
I'm enclosing check for $14.95 + 1.75 Shipping & Handling
for each copy ordered. (Texas Residents add $1.23 Tax)

Send to:_____

Address_____

_____

_____